The Bindings in the BONDAGE

Asetta Ramsey

© 2017 by Asetta Ramsey. All rights reserved.

No part of this book may be reproduced in any form, by any electronic or mechanical means (including photocopying, recording, or information storage and retrieval) without permission in writing from the author and publisher.

Cover Model: Dorothy Kinslow
Photographer: Ion Chiosea
Cover / Interior Design: HotBookCovers.com
Editing: Tamika Sims and Mairssa of inkpendiva.com

In Loving Memory

Of Rose and the Rose Beauty Supply
Family in Brooklyn, New York

Dedication

Dear God,

Thank you for saving my life and showing me what it really means to be loved and to love whole heartedly in everything I do.

To Professor Stoute, Thank you for being the best academic advisor, counselor, and teacher a college student could ever ask of. For always speaking life, passion, creativity, and purpose into me when my perspective was jaded.

To Angelic, Euclid, Rachel, Jessica and my whole HIRT family, thank you for keeping me in your prayers and in your hearts. Thank you Angelic for finding a way to manifest my visions and helping me with the foundation of my brand. Euclid thank you for being a friend and confidant and helping me heal through Christ with who I once was and who I am becoming. Rachel thank you for being the bomb lol. Thank you for late night laughs and encouragement. Thank you for shouting me out and pumping me up. Jessica thank you for speaking and awakening up the woman warrior in me through Christ.

To my Mother, Father, and both my Grandmothers, Thank you for being just who you are to me, fighters. I made a promise to each one of you, and I intend to keep it. I'll save the real speech when I receive my prestigious award like I dreamed.

To my immediate family and my extended family, I LOVE Y'ALL. Through all the ups and downs we have in our lifetime, although we feel alone in it sometimes, we've gone through the pain of struggling together. I'm so proud to be related to you all and I wouldn't trade you all or any of my experiences for nothing. I intend to keep pushing through and making you all proud.

To My best friend, Chu Baby (Avianca). Thank you for loving me beneath my surface wounds. I wasn't always the best of a friend to you in the beginning but I thank you for never leaving my side. Through thick, thin, right, wrong, good, bad, indifferent, winnings and struggles we have been through it all together. Thank you for 12 years of cemented friendship. I can't wait to see what the next 12 years are like.

To Ernesto, thank you for being there. Before this book no one knew I was struggling with bi-polar depression, but you lived it. You got to experience the ups and downs with me as your girlfriend of 10 plus years. I'm sorry for how I have treated you. I thank you for still loving me when others would have left. I never appreciated all that you were to me until after we broke up and I gave my life to Christ. Before you were my lover, you were my friend. I thank you for still being my friend. I love you so much and no matter where I go in life, I will never forget you. you will always have my heart.

To Latanya and Ms. Venus, thank you for loving me at my lowest. Thank you Latanya for helping me find my VOICE! Oh God girl you don't even know how hard of a task it was to find my voice in this world. I was timid and silent when it came to speaking my true feelings. I prayed for boldness and assertiveness. God used you to help me find it. NOW THAT IS A TRUE GIFT. You will never understand how much loving on you means to me. Ms. Venus thank you for giving me strength and teaching me how to keep my head up despite difficulties. You are my mother away from home. When I was broken and had no job, you made sure to check on me constantly. I love the way you embrace me. Thank you for keeping me dancing and laughing. Thank you for taking my mind off the bad things in my life. Thank you for loving me like I was one of your daughters.

To my Monte Co-workers, Roger, Rabbi Michael, Anne, and Charmaine thank you for listening to my story before it became a book. Thank you for praying for me and promoting me to anyone who would care to listen. You guys were my first audience, my first supporters. Thank you for believing in me and jumping in to push me closer to my dreams.

To Abdulla and Elijah, Abdulla thank you for pushing me to get out of the prison of my mind. For telling me to do this book when it was just a thought. You inspired me to get out of the prison of my mind for good while you were in the federal prison system. I love you Cheese and I can't wait until you come home. Rest in peace Elijah aka Bx Baller. I remember laughing, hanging out with you, and our conversations just about life. I feared for yours because you were everywhere but still in these streets. You knew you were meant to shine. I remembered you telling me your biggest fear of getting shot in the street and dying alone with no one by your side. How you wanted to leave the flashy street life sooner than later before it all caught up to you. You lost your life the same way you feared and you opened my eyes to want to live. I get teary-eyed when I think how short your beautiful life ended. With this book, your memory in me lives on. Thank you for apologizing for being mean to me as a kid growing up on Burnside.

To my Goddaughters Serenity and Kaliyah, my baby Camron, Davae and that boy Tayden. Thank you for loving Setta to no limit. Thank you for bringing me Joy in the times I spent with you. I'm happy to know that you guys are our future leaders. Setta love the kids' lol. I want you guys to have the best that life can offer. I sacrifice, work hard, and try to lead by example so that you can dare to dream big. Let no one tell you that you can't be something that you want to be or do something that has never been done. I'm living proof that anything you want in life is possible.

To my cousin Nay Nay (Kendall). They say you always save the best for last, but you are my first best, my last best, my everything. You're more than just my cousin you're my sister. There's nothing that I wouldn't do for you, no line that I won't cross. We have always been together. There's no Asetta without Kendall and vice versa. Two cousins navigating the world with each other. There's no secret left untold from one another, no battle we've haven't tackled hand in hand. You have always been there for me. I'm the oldest but you stepped up and have taken care of me since 18. From all the flashy parties, clothes, to going out and just having fun. You encouraged me to live a life that I wasn't living. You knew I wanted to be free to live for a long time. I thank you for bending over backwards to make sure it happened. I remember feeling below and inadequate around some of your high maintenance friends. You told me that everything wasn't always what it seemed. You told me not to believe the hype. You showed me the downside of what it really took sometimes to be that type of girl and how overall it wasn't worth it. You told me that the most important thing in life was being myself. I didn't have to be like them to be noticed, I just had to be Asetta. Asetta who danced, laughed, joked, and knew how to have a good time. I thank Tyshia Sharlena Bryant for giving birth to you. You don't understand how precious you are to me because I don't see you only for who you are but what you can become. Your mom was the glitter in my life and I thought that it would die when she did but it didn't. You are the glitter in my life. Everything beautiful in you reminds me of her. Everything good in you reminds me of how great God is in my life. I LOVE YOU BEYOND MEASURE, WORDS, AND LIFE. So many great things are going to happen in our futures, this is the first step, I know our mothers are so proud us. Straight to the top baby girl!

And if I forgot anyone because Lord knows I tried to remember everyone. THANK YOU.

Prologue

"TWO ARE BETTER THAN ONE... FOR IF THEY FALL, ONE WILL LIFT UP THE OTHER."
–ECCLESIASTES 4:9-10

"I am not prepared, but I am ready. I was once dead, but now I live."

Writing is my passion. It was brought to life through the pain of losing someone I loved dearly. God took my aunt away too soon, but I have come to learn that that was a part of His plan. My aunt had to leave so that God could ignite my passion. I struggled and went through the things I did, but that was a part of the plan too because while I went through my trials and tribulations physically, mentally, and emotionally, God allowed me to evolve spiritually through writing.

I have always felt different. I have always felt as if I was great and should be doing as such in the inside, but I was never great enough on the outside and I understand even better now, that that was because I was not meant to become a product of my environments, my environments were meant to become products of me. I love the Bronx, the borough itself, and the people that live in it.

Asetta Ramsey

I love the Bronx so much because here is where it is <u>BROKEN</u>, <u>LEFT</u>, <u>LOST</u>, and <u>FORGOTTEN</u>. <u>I LOVE BROKEN PEOPLE.</u> I have been broken. On earth, I will leave paper trails that subject me to and brand me as a person who suffers with bipolar depression. My medical records will stretch far beyond the horizon, but I was never crazy. God never designed me or anyone for that matter that way. I was <u>DEAD</u> and <u>LOST</u>. When you allow yourself to die and lose yourself amongst the beliefs of people telling you you're not smart enough, not good enough, not talented enough, the very opposite of how you felt <u>BEFORE</u> you started to believe their lies, because that's what they are, you get to a brokenness where you forfeit your rights to the endless possibilities of God's greatness.

    I died and forfeited my rights to greatness and roamed the earth lost, helpless, and hopeless. I blamed God for my circumstances because I was constantly stumbling when I should have taken accountability and blame for the decisions of my own actions. I became confused when I attached the ideas and opinions of everyone, but my own to me. I was frustrated because I <u>CHOSE</u> to do what was popular when it was indifferent to me. I was overwhelmed because my mind was not in agreement with my heart and soul.

    God showed up. He spoke healing to my heart where the damage cemented itself. I am a pusher. I was always pushing, but never satisfied or happy. I was always searching for something more because my heart desired and believed that there was more. My mind couldn't see or understand what my heart wanted because I was operating and maneuvering through life with thoughts that were not mine, labels that did not belong to me. I suffered tremendously because of this. It's okay though, because the beauty of suffering and pain is that I am not alone. Pain and suffering is relatable. It is the common ground for uncommon people.

PROLOGUE

WHEN DID YOU DIE?
WHEN DID YOU GIVE UP?
WHEN DID YOU BEND AND CONFORM TO THE LIES YOU WERE TOLD AS IF THEY WERE TRUTH?
WHEN DID YOU STOP BELIEVING IN GOD'S ENDLESS POSSIBILITIES?
WHEN DID YOU STOP BELIEVING IN YOU?

I was afraid to talk this way, to share my testimony with you. I am not what a Christian looks like, I didn't feel as if I was worthy of help. I was not raised in the church. I walk, talk and move different. I don't have a college degree or PhD, on how doctors and professionals view and study the mind, but I do know that through Jesus Christ I am healed.

I was chosen. I boldly believe that I don't suffer from a chemical imbalance in my brain, but a generational curse of negative thoughts and feelings, a poverty and broken mindset that God chose me to break and set free from.

God allowed me to go through struggles, grief, and turmoil. I call this the process. The process is meant to test you, and tug at your heart and your soul while you fight against the battles of your mind. You reach that place where after a while everything falls apart and it all goes black and dark. There seems to be no way out. You're all alone and everyone and anything that has ever influenced you, up until the point of darkness, is nowhere to be found. It's just you in your body with your thoughts and feelings breaking down. In that moment of breaking down, the only person left to give a try, or cry out for help is God. There is where He will be found and He will chisel the cement over your heart, shining His light in your darkness. Alone in the darkness with Him and only Him is where the real you is found.

God has given me my purpose. My purpose is to help you, like God has helped me by encouraging healing to your heart through my story. I share my story fearlessly because I have been prepared and built for this. My purpose is for the greater good, and the greater good is the Kingdom of God. Who is a part of the Kingdom of God?

It is you. You are apart of the Kingdom of God.

This is not a coincidence but an encounter. I am a blueprint designed and created by God to intercede in your life. My purpose is to uplift, motivate, and encourage you to wake up. You've been dead, sleeping, and lost for too long.

Do not give up on your dreams, passion, desires, and do not give up on yourself.

This message is for you if you're tired of being complacent in your life, when you feel you deserve and want more out of it. For the person who wants to challenge their thoughts and feelings of pain, suffering being all that life has got to offer them. For the person who's tired of failing by everyone else's standards. This message is for you if you want to be authentic, unique, and unapologetically you. I wish I had someone who could have helped me to do something about how I was feeling when I was this way. Someone that could relate to me. Hopefully for you in hearing my testimony I hope that your eyes, mind and heart are awakened and renewed. I wrote this book, my baby, as a gift to you. I hope my testimony in this book helps you to get inspired to start up or revisit a passion, desire, goal, or dream. I'm here to tell you that I know what it feels like to lose your mind and go insane trying to move to the ways of the world, hitting nothing but rock bottoms

PROLOGUE

multiple times over. I'm also here to tell you that once you hit those rock bottoms, there's nowhere else to go but up.

It's okay to be different, misunderstood, or not popular. It's okay to dare to do the unexpected, to dream bigger, to strive harder, to want to go further than the limits of those around you. It's okay to want to elevate. If you want to do all these things the right way and stay honest and true to yourself, I want you to try to change your perspective on how you've been operating in your own life. I'm not here to force you into believing in the God that I serve, God would never approve of that. I'm just saying that as a non-believer once, and even when I did believe, I hadn't really known Him, Consider God in your life decisions when you find yourself at a low like I did.

I'm not saying that tomorrow you will get holy, sanctified, and start preaching the Gospel either. That's where you will fail. God does not work like that and that's how I used to think. I'm simply saying that when you make a decision, while you're going through obstacles and hurdles in life like I was, like I still am, consider Him by thinking of you. Tell Him what's on your mind and in your heart before you consider the thoughts and opinions of other people who don't think or have the same aspirations as you. Consider Him in your lonely hours when you need help and don't see a way out of <u>YOUR</u> problems.

Consider Him when you start to doubt your abilities. Consider Him when things get hard and you find yourself wanting to take the easier route. Consider Him when your mind is not in agreement with your heart and soul. God moves through your soul to condition your heart, but only if you open your heart and allow Him to move in you. I hope if this message ever finds you dead, lost or broken, you decide to take power over your own life and declare

Asetta Ramsey

to live and come out of agreement with everything your mind, friends, family, or people have ever said you were, are, or ever will be TODAY.

"WHEN I TOOK MY POWER BACK I WROTE THIS BOOK, WHEN I WROTE THIS BOOK, I THOUGHT OF YOU. THANK YOU FROM THE BOTTOM OF MY HEART FOR READING."

-Words from the Author

Asetta Ramsey

Chapter One

*"A **THOUSAND** times we **DIE** in one **LIFE**. We **CRUMBLE**, **BREAK** and **TEAR APART** until the **LAYERS** of **ILLUSION** are **BURNED AWAY** and all That is **LEFT**, is the **TRUTH** of **WHO** and **WHAT** We **REALLY ARE**."* - Teal Scott

To simply put it, I laid there. Thoughtless in mind, but endless in spirit. Like when you have so much to say to a crush, but once you open your mouth to profess your undying love, nothing comes out. I laid there, on the queen size air mattress that I shared with my two sisters as I watched the roaches scatter the ceiling. I tried to understand them. How could such ugly creatures exist? How come they didn't coincide with the laws of gravity? Why had they not fallen when the world as I had seen it was upside down? What I would have given to not be human at all, to have just simply been a roach. Tears streamed down my face as I let the thought sink in. Reaching to disarm my five o'clock alarm, I noticed that I had been up for three hours in the dark watching roaches crawl the living room ceiling and listening to the sounds of the hood. A police siren in the distance, a gunshot following it. I always second guessed, wondering to myself if my brother and uncle came home earlier that night. In "The Browns," where I resided, the wee hours of the mornings belonged to the birds. The pigeons claimed the dead silence if a body didn't.

I got up, called the sick hotline for my job to let them know that I wasn't coming into work today. This had been my fourth call out this month. I was sure to get a write-up, suspension from work, or worse, terminated. In the bathroom as more tears rolled down my face, I cracked the only smile I'd seen in months. This was my life at work. I was running from work patterns considered disorderly conduct according to my job's rules and regulations. I cringed at the words, "Go get a delegate" every time I walked into the main manager's office. So much so, that I avoided walking directly past his office and if I had to, I held my breath. If he didn't know I was there breathing in his vicinity, I would not exist for the day. He terrified me. One time I was for sure that he did not like me or better yet that I did not like him because of how he talked down to people, to me, especially. Maybe he did know, but because I held my breath so long while he humiliated me to keep from crying or, worse, to keep from telling him that I was going to get my father to fuck him up if he ever disrespected me again, I became passively invisible. Holding my breath allowed me to disappear. I no longer cared about work though, consequences didn't matter to me. I'd lost the need to work let alone get up for it. The problems I was facing were staring back at me as I wiped my stained face for the millionth time.

My family was homeless. My mother did not own an apartment anymore. We lost the home we'd known for 12 years due to my mother's financial struggles to support a home by herself with five children. She never told me that things were bad until they surpassed bad and got damaging. That's my madre though, the

CHAPTER ONE

strongest woman I know. It's always been me and her, you know? My role transformed into that of a son who becomes a man after his father dies and steps up to the plate to take his place and uphold the family.

  I stepped up when our fathers stepped out. I tried as best as I could to brace myself and help when mommy sat me down and gave me the VIP velvet rope special into her club of catastrophes. She was running the club all by herself. She was the owner, bouncer, bartender, waitress, busser, Dj, and the hottest artist at the time making a debut appearance to the club. When she gave me access to her dancefloor so that I could dance the night away, I stood there in the dark on shattered glass hearing her say, "Shine my star," but I could not, her lighting was missing, and no one was in control of the lights in this dark ass club.

  I emptied out my bank account three times to help mommy with the rent to save our home, but after one too many, "one shot deals" and other government subsidy program denials, we lost our home. To add fuel to the fire, we were burning alive in, mommy lost her Section 8. Section 8 was like gold to low-income families such as ours. A housing voucher that was needed for all, but given to so few. This was one of very few rental assistances provided to low-income families so that they could afford housing. I love New York, but the truth of the matter is that being classified as "low-income" or "middle class" in New York still meant you were poor. There is no middle man, you're either poor without a job, still poor with a job or wealthy. We were poor for certain. The very reason why I hated shopping downtown on 34th street, sight-seeing down 42nd street, or hitting up a good eatery like *Chutney and Co.* on a good pay day in SoHo was because the very things that I loved that I could do in the city I lived in, reminded me of how much I couldn't really afford it, which made me come to the realization that I did not fit in where I wanted to belong. My special moments were luxuries, but to those who lived in those areas, "The Wealthy" it was life. It was just another day, like walking in Central Park.

Tourists added to that agony as I watched in awe while they marveled at the sky scrapers. They stood amongst the hustle and bustle of the city's mixed people. I was angry with them because while they praised the land known as Manhattan, with dreams and hopes of maybe one day really making it here or getting to tell their loved ones in foreign countries that they visited the "Big Apple." The land of opportunity, their New York that was portrayed in movies and on TV wasn't mine. There was the Bronx inside the "rotten apple," The bottom of the barrel. Where the only skyscrapers known were called projects and the hustle and bustle of the borough was running and dodging bullets when all you wanted to do was enjoy a cookout with friends and family in Crotona park on a beautiful day. The wealthy never come out here, here is where nobody belonged.

Knock, knock, knock!

My grandmother is right on time. I know that it's now six am because my grandmother uses the bathroom every time at this hour in the morning. Unaware of the whole hour I spent in the bathroom mirror crying, I let her in. Disgusted at the sight of her and the stench of her skin that was coated in alcoholic poisoning, she greets me with words that heavily resemble her appearance, *"Get the fuck out of my house squatter."* These words managed to slip from under her breath faster than I could close the door behind her. That was the reality of her, my alcoholic severely depressed grandmother. We didn't get along at all. Every ounce of love in me had converted into the very energy used for the hatred I had for her. I

CHAPTER ONE

hated what she had become when the memories of joy and love I had for her clouded my childhood past. I did not recognize the spirit occupying the body of the woman I once held so dear to my heart. My real grandmother, the one I knew before the alcoholic episodes and depression, died and left her body sometime after I was 11 years old. What was left was a walking bottle of vodka with my grandmother's face implanted on the broken seal. I disowned her flesh when I mentally laid her true spirit to rest in my mind.

I usually had a more painful derogatory remark in response to whatever came out of the old lady's miserable mouth, but today was different. Today, I let her words cut me deep as I kept my eyes to the floor acknowledging that she would be the last person to see me again and her words would be the last spoken I would hear from a family member. I'd gotten dressed quietly and spoke no words for fear that I would wake my mother who I did not want to disturb or try to stop me from what I planned for the day. As I stepped outside the early seven am air hit me like pine needles to my face.

It was one of the many bad blizzard days in New York City. I had not remembered it to snow that day. Truth of the matter is, I hadn't remembered anything lately. My mind was unstable and the only thing that had been constant was thoughts of death. I decided that I didn't want to live to see twenty-five, one week before my birthday. How did I get here? I was once a jolly and jubilant 18-year-old who had the ambition of a million women to do anything and everything that was set in my mind and embedded in my heart, and no one could tell me otherwise. Where did she go? I blinked and went from eighteen to twenty-four years old in what seemed like a matter of minutes compared to years feeling confused and frustrated. Where did the time go so fast? I often contemplated with myself. I felt like my fountain of youth was running dry soon. Yeah,

Asetta Ramsey

I get it that I was only twenty-four years old and I had so much more living to do, but that was just it. Six years of my life had already surpassed me and I made no progress in my life and what little progress that I did make I had nothing to show for it. I would blink again and I would be thirty just like that. I was pressing for time I had lost, but time lost is time never to be seen or found again.

Since I couldn't get a grip on this life that was given to me, I no longer wanted to be a part of it. Of all the human beings that roamed the earth, why was I chosen? In my heart I felt unaccomplished, as if something was missing in my life. The very thing that sparked the fire and ignited my soul. The very thing that gave me invincible wings and allowed me to soar beyond my wildest desires in life. I'd lost sight of my dreams and couldn't figure out the purpose of my life. I knew that I was supposed to be a woman of great virtue and success. I was supposed to be a powerful woman that many could one day look up to, but look at me. I lived in one of the poorest and most dangerous neighborhoods in the Bronx. Everyday living with the reality that we would never make it out of this building because of the high cost of rent and every day that was lived in the ghetto, was cemented confirmation that I would never get out of here. If this was the life I was meant to live I didn't want it. This life was unfair to me. I should have amounted to so much more; my life should have had more meaning.

I didn't want to become a female ghetto stereotype, a statistic. I didn't want to become pregnant like so many women I knew at a young age and be complacent with my living environment. My world was no place for me to continue living in, let alone bring a child into. I just couldn't figure out my life anymore or who I was in it. I was going crazy replaying and overthinking the stages of my life that brought me to the very decisions of ending it today. If

CHAPTER ONE

I wasn't being talked down to at work, I was being talked about. My kindness had been taken advantage of by the very co-workers I considered friends. At home, there was no escape to peace with the nine of us that resided in the two-bedroom apartment my grandmother's soul once lived in. This home, in this neighborhood, in this borough, I'd grown up in was all that I'd known.

I feared this reality for other young women sharing the same personal backgrounds as me, if not worse. I was a prime witness to the women and men that gave up on life to remain residents of a neighborhood that didn't love the people it birthed. The thought sat unsettlingly in my soul. The loss of friends to the grave or the penitentiary chasing fast money or gun-violence made me livid. I had younger siblings whose lives I feared for every day. I didn't want to lose my only brother to a bullet or my sisters to prostitution. I knew what it felt like to lose a friend, that I considered a brother. I was once pregnant at a young age and got an abortion, I entertained men for their money, I participated in illegal activities and suffered the consequences chasing fast money. I did not want my siblings to be anything like me, I wanted them to be better.

I was tired of fighting the everyday struggles of living and surviving just enough to make it through the day. Only to repeat it all over again tomorrow. I didn't want tomorrow to come. Tomorrow meant another day of staring at the sky from the pit of the rock bottom I'd succumbed to. I was searching for a way out of the hells of a life I was force fed, and thoughts of suicide became the supreme need to fulfill. The iniquitous state of my mind was alive and in full effect. I knew what was happening to me was more than serious, but I couldn't stop it, I no longer knew how to.

My plan was to drop all my classes for the final time. I had been a freshman at Bronx Community College for five years now.

Asetta Ramsey

Yeah, you heard me correctly. For five years, I'd been a freshman at my community college. I enrolled in school with no way of paying the remaining two-thousand-dollar tuition left for that semester. I'd only been to class three times, the semester started in January and it was now March. I was too distracted for school. I was a half-asser who had the full potential to get shit done. I wanted to be there so bad, college was the only way out for me. College was the key to success, but it was slipping out of my grasp, my hands weren't strong enough to hold on. I could barely start college, let alone complete it. I felt like a failure, a useless body taking up space. India Arie once said, *"There's no substitute for the truth, it either is or it isn't,"* and truth was everything was falling apart. I had lost all control.

    I was hopeless. The thought of God giving me life to live it the way I was living made me hate Him and myself even more. I was ready to give up. At least I knew the pain would cease, these feelings I felt about myself wouldn't exist anymore. I was willing do anything to make the pain stop.

    I was probably better off dead. I thought on the bus ride to school.

    I probably would have ended up working at a job I hated for the rest of my life, in debt up to my eyeballs, unable to live how I dreamed.

    Probably silly girl, are you not at the peak of this mountain?

    An inner voice said to me. All you have to do is jump off, do yourself the favor and jump off Asetta, the agony, oh, the agony.

    "Alright!" I yelled out loud on the crowded Bx32 bus as it pulled up to stop across the street from my school.

    I'd zoned out, completely forgetting my surroundings, as I

CHAPTER ONE

watched confused passengers turn their heads in my direction. I clenched my coat hood tighter for dear life as I bum rushed my way off the back of the bus.

"Even Rosa Parks should be ashamed of me," I said to myself as I crossed the street.

If I was going to bum rush, my black ass should have did it all the way to the front of the bus.

I stood in front of my school as I watched students and professors going in and coming out of the campus until the racing of my heart slowed down to a pace that I could take the next step with.

I repeated the plan over to myself, *"Go in, drop your classes, take the back entrance of the school straight to the Hudson River, jump in, don't think, Asetta. Not a second more, just jump."*

This plan was concrete. I didn't know how to swim so if I began to drown putting up a fight would be impossible. The Hudson River's filthy and murky waters would swallow me whole and regurgitate my lifeless body to be found days later, if anyone ever found me. I couldn't half ass this, this was solid. It's funny how complete and whole planning my death made me feel. I couldn't accomplish anything, but I was determined to get this done. I didn't question my motives because it felt right.

I awaited my advisor to call me to her office. Once in the confinements of her space, I tried desperately to pull up any ounce of energy left in me to force a smile and casual conversation. I wasn't very good at it.

"Professor Stoute, I'm here today because I want to drop all my classes," I said,

"This business management major isn't working out for me, at the moment, and I'm running into financial problems where I simply just can't afford school right now. I feel like such a failure."

I waited for Professor Stoute to quickly move me through the system and send me to the designated wing to finalize my request, but she stared at me intently and proceeded to put her glasses on. I became instantly uncomfortable as tears strolled down my face.

Fuck! I said annoyed, because she was doing what no one was, she was observing me, she was seeing through me.

"You are a writer. You should not be here in my office when I know and you know that every major you have come across is not the one for you," she continued,
"Why are you fighting your natural talent to become something else other than what you truly are? Why have you not once changed your major to journalism? I just don't understand it,"
Professor Stoute said bewildered.

We had always had conversations about my writing and the books we read. We shared inspiring stories and intriguing thoughts on how we viewed the world, where we stood in it and the dreams we had that were alive in it. I loved her dearly. Professor Stoute embraced creativity, and dared to be different, I admired her greatly for that.

"It's too late for all that professor," I said dryly, "I've already wasted so much time I'd have to start from the bottom and writing isn't cool. No one's rushing to the book stores to pick up poetry books. Writing isn't making money for me right now. I need the money now."

I said this wondering how in the world she couldn't see it from my point of view.

"All money isn't good money." She said sternly. "If you have talent, and I know you are more than talented, I've read your writing. In what you do, you don't have to chase the money Asetta,

CHAPTER ONE

the money will come to you," her words lingered in the air for a while. "You don't want to be stuck at some job that you absolutely hate woulda, coulda, shoulda, but didn't and unhappy. You should be doing the very thing that makes you happy." I paused at the thought of what she said.

Boom boom… boom boom… There was a tapping in my soul.

She was right, but I just couldn't believe her. I couldn't interpret what she was saying and apply it to my life. It was too late and I came to the conclusion to absolutely stick to my decision. "Professor Stoute never lived one day in my shoes; she's giving false hope to people like me because she likes my character. My character doesn't pay the bills.

Checkmate, I said in my head. I wasn't going to allow Professor Stoute to have the one up on me.

"I want to ask you something though before I drop your classes," she said to me.

There was ten seconds of complete silence. Ten seconds that determined life or death. Ten seconds to be here, ten seconds to be gone, ten whole seconds.

"I want you to schedule an appointment with the school's Counselor. From the looks of things, I don't know what's going on, but I think you should talk to someone."

I've been talking… I thought in my head as I stared at her blankly.

"To someone other than me," she said instantly as if she heard what I was thinking, *"I'm serious."* She stood there lightly tapping her leg with her pen still waiting for a reaction out of me.

"Okay I'll go make an appointment," I said sadly. I followed Professor Stoute down the hall, into the staircase to the second floor. The whole walk I didn't know what was worse, the fact

that I was lying to myself because I went to schedule an appointment I had no intentions of following through with, or that I was lying to Professor Stoute in having her think that she was helping me. I was still going to kill myself, I just did what was needed to get her out the way.

"Please come follow up with me after you make your appointment before you go Asetta," Professor Stoute nodded firmly as she squeezed my shoulder.

And with that she was gone, I would never see her again. I signed my name on the clipboard as I awaited the secretary to give me a date to attend. The last thing I'd ever put my signature on, I thought. There was a sudden ringing in my ear that shifted through my whole body. I grabbed my coat as I bolted to the woman's restroom. All of a sudden, I was gasping for air, my heart raced rapidly as my palms became sweaty. It was happening again. I couldn't explain what was actually happening to me or even knew where this feeling was coming from, but when it came it hit me with such a vengeance. All I could do was rub my sweaty hands down the sides of my pants and wheeze while the tears flowed endlessly. Once this feeling passed it left me exhausted and in so much pain. I contemplated the bar less window to jump out of, but from the size of the fall I'd most likely walk away with broken bones if not brain damage.

"Fuck this shit. I'm out right now!" I headed back down the hallway to the secretary's office to grab the rest of my belongings.

"I have to do this some other time miss, thank you for your time, but I have to go!" I said to the secretary with the nastiest attitude.

I was angry and that fueled me to run and jump in that river with full force. I was going to Olympic dive into that motherfucker if it was the last thing I'd do.

CHAPTER ONE

"Wait Ms. Ramsey!" the secretary said timidly.

"I was waiting for you to return; the Counselor is available to see you now. Her 1 o'clock canceled."

"Asetta, I'm the school's counselor can you please let me take your coat and come with me to my office? I won't take up much of your time I promise. I'm so very sorry to have had you waiting, but I need you to calm down please."

She was reaching for me to give her my coat as she spoke to me in the kind of tone a White mother uses to talk to her bad ass tantrum throwing kid in the grocery store.

How condescending of her to talk to me like that

I thought as I still clenched my belongings, but found myself raising my arm to give her my coat because at the same time, there was something also soothing about her voice, something that was pacifying me from losing it right where I stood.

I followed the counselor to her office. Once in, she motioned for me to have a seat on the sofa as she took a seat at her desk. I stood still.

"You're welcome to whatever snacks I have here, there's M&M's, Twizzlers, fine chocolate...."

The list went on and on as I stood there watching each location of candy that she pointed to, I was convinced her office was donated from Willy Wonka himself.

"I'm diabetic, and I don't want any fucking chocolate," I screamed! Tears filling up in the wells of my eyes, I was going to overflow.

Hold it in Asetta hold it till the river... I can't, I can't, I'm trying.

In between fighting myself against my sub-conscious in my head and desperately trying not to lose it in front of the counselor, she now standing firmly grounded at her desk, locked in dead with my eyes and with such fervor said,

"Asetta what is it that you want, right here right now, what is the problem?"

What is it that you want?

What is it that you want?

The words echoed swirling around me like ribbon twirlers.

"I-I," my lips trembling, tears cascading down my face endlessly, and then it happened. From deep within the belly of my soul I let out a screech so painful and piercing my knees buckled and I spread to the floor.

"I just want to be happy, I'm so tired."

I scrunched into fetal position as I lay on the floor while the counselor knelt to my side.

I laid there crumbling, breaking and tearing apart as the hidden layers of pain and despair I'd endured my whole life seeped from my lifeless body. Each agonizing bellow cutting me down to size until all that was left was the dead silence of me.

Chapter Two

DREAMS VS. REALITY

HER ARRIVAL

Writing came as naturally to me as a mother birthing through labor pains.
Pushing hard, panting breathlessly, bleeding,
Until the very second of the minute within the hour
became one with my soul.
My baby born beauteous in all its calamity.
Sturdy lungs that cry out and swaddle me like music to my ears.
Pain I've just endured to get my baby here,
a distant memory,
as I bask in the glory of all that feels good and makes me feel free.
My baby has been born,
And I have just been born again.

-Asetta Ramsey

Asetta Ramsey

That was how writing made me feel, it allowed me to be free. It all started when I was eight years old. My love for writing was birthed through pain. I lost my aunt Tyshia Sharlena Bryant to heart failure, Mother's Day, May 10^{th,} 1998. My childhood innocence walked out the back door freely to abduction when she died. My aunt was my world. She was like my second mom only cooler. My aunt took me everywhere she went, with my cousin Kendall, who was two years younger than me. As a trio, we were inseparable. One of the fondest memories of my aunt was going to the corner store with her so that she could buy me some snacks to eat outside. Fifty cent icees, a quarter water, fruit roll up, and chips gave a seven-year-old like me popularity and instant fame. The more sweets you stepped out back with to share, the cooler you became. As we left the store to return back to the apartment building, some random guy was checking her out from his car while driving. He stood parked in the middle of the street for so long and watched her so close as we crossed the street, that he caused major traffic. I mean the kind of traffic they bring helicopters for when there's a huge crash. The line of cars stretched far for so long that I was in awe. My eyes twinkled at her as she looked down holding my hand and smiled at me. It was then in that very moment, as I Kool-Aid smiled back to her, squeezing her hand, that I knew that the world seen her just as stunningly beautiful as I did. She had that very same effect on me. I could stare at her all day. She was so alluring, and I was extremely glad that she was mine.

With great joy came an even greater suffering. My aunt became sick July 1997 and after her first cardiac arrest, she was never the same again. It broke my heart tremendously to see her non-responsive. She no longer had control of her body, her eyes wandered. I felt in my heart that she not being able to speak, on top

CHAPTER TWO

of everything else, could still see and understand us. When my cousin Vellina said, "Eww," as my grandmother wiped saliva from my aunt's face, she frowned, so I knew inside of me she could hear us. I scolded my cousin in my head at her insensitive remark, but she was only six. Her brain wasn't grasping the severity. Though I was seven, I was really twenty-seven in spirit and fully aware of what was going on. I visited aunty as often as grandma allowed my cousin and me. We told her everything that happened in school as we laid beside her. My grandmother crying quietly in the corner as she pretended to look elsewhere. My grandmother gave everything to be strong for us and I felt deeply saddened for her. In our hearts, besides my baby cousin, I think we all had a sense that she was going to leave us and in knowing so was the biggest, hardest, driest pill to swallow.

Close to Mother's Day the following year in arts and crafts at school, we got to make flower corsages that your moms could wear. I chose that year to make my flower corsage for my aunt. It was beautiful and in my favorite color purple. I'd also hand made a card to go along with my gift for her. I was so eager and excited to give it to her. I'd spent a lot of time and effort perfecting her gift. This moment was big for me and so very important. I planned to tell her in her ear my feelings of her dying. I wanted to tell her how much I really loved her and that it was okay if she wanted to go to Heaven because I liked her better when she could speak. I would tell her that I would forever take care and watch over Kendall. I wanted to reassure her that I would never forget her, that my love for her would last always and forever as I placed her corsage on her arm. I wanted to say goodbye.

Mother's Day came, but we never made it to her. My aunt passed away that morning as we packed our gifts preparing to go see her. Death hit home hard as my cousin and I held each other in her room and cried. She cried for her mom and I cried for her. I cried, painfully, for the aunt I loved like my mother. I cried for the beauty she was, for the glitter she was to me that made my world sparkle. I made sure that I brought my corsage and card to her wake. I walked the two steps up winded as I struggled to make it up to her casket. They were the hardest two steps of my life. Her body felt cold and hard as I tied her corsage around her arm. I kissed her cheek and told her I loved her as I lost all control of my feelings. Screaming at the top of my lungs, my grandfather had to pry me off her body in her casket. As I was being damn near dragged out of the funeral home tears falling continuously, I envisioned her as an angel wearing my corsage. I wanted her to stand out in Heaven. I could see her in all white and gold with the most elegant purple flower ever. Her flower would be real in Heaven and no one would have that corsage on so that would make her extra special. God would know that on earth she was highly favored.

I fell into such a deep depression when I lost my aunt. I talked less and cried more. This pain I carried in me was so deeply rooted that I couldn't tell anyone what I was feeling.

I could barely find the words to speak because this kind of pain was not told, but felt. Overwhelmed from holding it all in, I felt the words rising up in me like air bubbles in soda searching for a release. I picked up a notebook, turned to a clean piece of loose leaf paper and let my emotions bleed. In the time that I was writing down the unmentionable feelings trapped in my heart, there was this sense of temporary relief from it all. An almost euphoria. It was like I was able to dislocate these painful memories that made me feel and put it somewhere else. I no longer had to carry it. I was pulling the pain out of my heart and trapping it in the lines of my

CHAPTER TWO

journal. Writing provided the comfort I so desperately longed for from coping with the empty presence of my aunt. Writing was my escape from real life to an entirely new dimension of love, sorrow, mystery, and happiness..

Overtime, writing became one with me, and I with it, like breathing. I'd become skillfully talented in this art of expression. Poetry was my first love. Then I moved my way into memoirs, short stories, and essays. I knew that I was gifted with something that not only made me feel good, but when I read aloud, the voice I was allowed to give to words that had so much meaning to me, captivated whoever listened. Many people could feel what I was saying while I used very few words to say it. From that moment on I wanted to make a career out of writing. I wanted to write for newspapers and magazines. I wanted to be an author, a poet, as well as a teacher. If it meant I would never have to stop writing or sharing, I was willing to do it.

I was a dreamer. I dreamed big and hard. I dreamed far and wide. I day dreamed a lot about the famous woman I would become. I knew somehow that I was destined to shine without a shadow of doubt, I felt so set up for greatness on the inside. I dreamed of being on Oprah and meeting my all-time favorite poet Maya Angelou prior to her death. Ms. Angelou would present me with the Nobel Peace Prize award for a stunning poem or great piece of literature that touched millions. I practiced my cursive signature for book signings. I wrote short speeches on receipt papers and pretended that I didn't know I was the chosen one at literary award ceremonies. I thanked everyone on my make believe list as I pretended my mom was looking straight at me from the crowd, and my aunt from Heaven. Tears rolling down my face as I told everyone how it was such an honor to be here. How humbly blessed

Asetta Ramsey

I was to be sharing this experience with them. I had reoccurring dreams of me standing at a podium speaking in front of millions of people. My dreams felt so real and magical to me. I just couldn't wait to achieve them.

    It came as no surprise to my mom that when it was time to pick my top 10 schools to attend for high school, my first-choice school was the Bronx Academy of Letters. It was as if this school waited until I was ready to go to high school to exist. This school was specifically made for me. The Bronx Academy of Letters was a new Urban League school that had just completed its first full year by the time I applied. The school was built on the model that: Students who can express themselves clearly in writing can do better in any path they chose in life. In order to attend this school, I had to write an essay and once selected attend summer bridge. Summer bridge was a series of engaging break the ice activities so that you got to know your new peers and staff. I aced it all and was accepted to the high school of my dreams. I was so thrilled because this was the first step into the next chapter of my life. This school would shape and mold me into the person I dreamed to become.

    I would love to tell you that my high school experience was nothing short of amazing. I would love to recall all the wonderful things I did, the beautiful friends I made, and all the tools I gained to become this awesome person I am today. I laugh at the thought because for me high school was a blur. The four years I attended were anything, but sweet. My grades plummeted. I would cut school sometimes, I was sexually active, and smoking marijuana. On the days I was in school when it came to paying attention, I checked out. I slept a lot, refused to participate effectively in class, and gained a new title as class clown when I decided to be alert.

CHAPTER TWO

The joke was on me though and nothing was funny at all, my home was changing. My stepfather, the man we loved, feared and respected all at once, left my mother after being in a relationship with her for more than ten years. I didn't know what was worse the fact that he married and conceived a child with a woman not much older than me, or that he wasn't man enough to tell my mom because she had to find out on her own. The news devastated my mother. her hopes of marrying the man she gave four children to over the years, going through the ups and downs with him, crushing her dreams of becoming his wife was all too much to fathom.

My household was disrupted. Mommy was left struggling to support and provide for her children. Our sibling bond began to go sour and divide. We all argued and fought more. He deserted us and we weren't prepared for his absence. My siblings tried to make sense of it all, but I was just trying to get away. Go to a place where I could numb the pain. I knew then like I knew when I was eight, that when devastation hit home I had to be strong. I knew I had to prepare myself for what was to come. Mommy couldn't do this alone; she couldn't survive on her own. It was time to grow up. My last year of high school I became an adult. I graduated with regents' honors by the skin of my teeth. I did what I needed to do to get shit done. No crying, no whining, I had no time for that. Failure was not an option. I knew that if I failed, I'd set the bar for failure for my siblings. They could hold over mommy's head that I didn't finish high school, so when they felt like giving up, it would be ok to do so.

I didn't want that to happen, I didn't want to be responsible for their actions.

I left the Bronx Academy of Letters with bittersweet memories. Since mommy couldn't afford them, I had no graduating pictures to show that I existed in high school once. I decided to pretend that high school didn't exist and chose to forget it all. I could forget that I existed in that time so that there was no need to remember or reminisce. I wouldn't have to compare the goals or dreams I once had against the actual turnout. I was ashamed to re-live any events from high school. I was sinking in the quicksand of the realness I was living in. Those dreams of writing and living beyond my wildest desires had died. Writing was nothing more than just a hobby I told myself. My stepfather was right. He'd asked me once, before he left so abruptly out of our lives;

"Asetta," he said as he sat across from me at the dining room table.

"What are you going to do as a career for your future, who do you want to be?"

"I want to write, journalism maybe." I said smiling with glee.

'That's good Asetta, but have you ever considered something else more than just writing, another career maybe?"

Another career? I was puzzled. I had never considered any other career than writing.

"I don't really think writing is really a career for someone like you, think about it." I looked on as he proceeded to break it down. He told me how it would take me years to get to where I wanted to go, and how I would have to start from the bottom. I knew that his intentions were to mean well and that all he was trying to do was to steer me in the right direction, but his advice was in the opposite direction of all I had known, all I aspired to be.

"You need to think about a realistic career that will make you money and lots of it," he said.

CHAPTER TWO

"Writing isn't going to do that for you Asetta, I'm telling you," I believed him.

I believed especially more than ever. Every time mommy shed a silent tear at night, every month the overdue rent notices were slid under the door, and as I noticed it became harder to keep the fridge stocked, the demand for money became what was more important. Reality kicked me down hard and made me realize that my dreams didn't match my bank account, so I gave up on them and traded in my dreams of writing for fast cash in needed times.

Asetta Ramsey

DEARLY DEPARTED

Reality took my baby from me.
Snatched her right up out of my hands after the delivery.
Being born again doesn't mean you're born free.
Sign these papers and let her be.
An unfit mother life labeled me.
I cannot raise you,
I can barely raise me.
I have struggled in this world
like my mother and her mother before.
You deserve so much better,
maybe more than me.
the thought alone saddens me.
I sign the dotted line dejectedly.
Refusing to let failure raise you,
like it raised me.

-Asetta Ramsey

Chapter Three

DON'T BELIEVE THE HYPE

"Sometimes our <u>THOUGHTS</u> are backed by so much <u>INSECURITY</u>, that they create <u>LIES</u> we <u>BELIEVE</u>."
– Anonymous

High school was over and done with. I set my dreams aside like unfinished books on dusty book shelves hoping to return to them soon, deep down knowing that there's the slightest possibility that I may never return to pick up that same book again. I took the advice of my step father and enrolled into community college, where I majored in nursing. I wasn't ecstatic about going to community college at all. I wish that I didn't take high school for granted and did really good academically. I wish I did well enough to get a scholarship to an excellent college. I dreamed of experiencing the "college campus life" in some prestigious school in a state far away from home. It was far too late for thoughts like that though. I quickly brushed them under the rug and put my best foot forward.

Asetta Ramsey

I attended college with new dreams of becoming a registered nurse, or so I thought. Nursing was the wave. Besides my stepfather's indication to become one, everyone I knew was going to school for nursing, medical coding, or to become a physician assistant. Working in the medical field was at the top of the majority's list and like my mother used to say whenever there was a dispute about anything amongst my siblings and I, majority rules.

I'd done a little research on my career, as in Google search top paying jobs in New York City, and saw that registered nurses came in at number four and made a pretty penny. According to what kind of nurse you wanted to be and in what location you worked in, you could go really far with nursing. I wasn't all the way sold on becoming a registered nurse until I got the chance to announce it to friends and family. Everyone was so proud of me. I was told my future was very promising. I would be making a large amount of money, and, overall, I made the right decision on what to do with my life.

All the hype of how good I would do as a nurse and how truly proud my family and friends were of me got me excited. I felt accepted for sure. Okay it wasn't what I truly wanted to do, but becoming a nurse gave me substance. Something tangible that I could hold on to outside of my dreams that allowed me to fit in and be regular with my friends and family.

"If this makes everyone around me happy, that means that I can be happy, right?"

I thought back to the responses I received when my days were filled with dreams of writing and besides my mom's constant support; the reactions I received were far from the same. I let the thoughts go feeling very validated and important that I was doing something everyone approved of. Feeling like I could fit in allowed me to look at my circumstances differently.

CHAPTER THREE

While everyone was so thrilled I made a popular choice, I was thrilled to be accepted and to up my finances. The average median based salary for registered nurses was $77,940. Forget the fact that I didn't even care to know what a salary was; the money was what really reeled me in. I wanted to get paid. I'd be making money I'd never touched before. Making money meant I could save my immediate family, protect and provide generously for them. I could make a wealthy life for myself and future family. Becoming a nurse meant I had the opportunity to travel. Because nursing was an occupation that would always be in constant demand. If I wanted to leave my home town and become a nurse somewhere like Hawaii, because I loved warm climates, there was little to nothing that could hold me back if I chose to do so. The best and I mean the best feeling of them all, would be the day I could walk into a store and buy all the expensive things my heart desired without having to take one look at the price tag. I would reminisce of the countless window shopping days, times when I loved something but had to put it back because I couldn't afford it. The flip between having nothing and having it all, that was the beauty of what I wanted to live for. I wanted the "come up." I would no longer be the girl who was made fun of that wore the hand me downs and knock offs. The only problem I wanted to have was whether I wanted to pay for my expenses with cash or card.

I dreamed that nursing would give me that kind of power, all while doing what I've always done best, caring for and helping people. I was naturally a healer. I loved lending people in need a helping hand. Showing compassion for people from my heart was effortless and brought me great joy.

I can really do this! I thought to myself, *it's not too far-fetched, I don't have to do too much, and the least I would have to worry about is getting used to blood and a little math here and there.*

I did not want to set my expectations too high.

Whatever was a little hard would get easier if I kept the mindset that if I was persistent in learning it, that would make me consistent in achieving it. Boy, was I wrong! After about a month and a half of school, I realized that I was way in over my head. I hated every math class with a passion. I also hated science just as much as I hated math and the two classes went hand in hand. I signed up for tutoring to get help with the two subjects, but it was too much of a hardship for me.

I was unaware that the nursing program I was attending was not only one of the top programs college wise, but very competitive. Any grade lower than a B+ was unacceptable and caused you to be kicked out of the program. I was a C+ student with B- tendencies. I could try my hardest to make the grade, but keeping it was another story. I hadn't taken the time out to realize that my perception of nursing and what it actually took to become one were two different understandings. I was focused on the rewards of becoming a nurse and not the actual diligence it took to get there. My mind made up, I dropped all my classes immediately before they had any real chance to affect my GPA. I took on a series of different jobs to help mommy with some of the house's expenses while in and out of school and to keep busy. I needed to keep money in my pockets, but each unhappy job made me want to drop my jobs like I'd dropped my classes.

Dropping classes became a sport I was excelling in. Every year from 2009 until 2013, I had a new major. My second major was Liberal Arts and, believe it or not, I was pretty happy about it. I found myself doing a lot of writing and getting into psychology

CHAPTER THREE

classes. I loved it. That feeling was short lived after I told a family member when asked about my nursing major.

"Liberal Arts isn't a real major. You know that, right, Asetta?" My cousin told me as we discussed my decisions.

"It's a little bit of everything, every subject tied into one which basically means you're majoring in you-don't-know-what-you-want-to-do-as-a-career."

My cousin didn't know, but those words sliced me like a paper cut, and paper cuts hurt extremely bad.

"I hadn't thought about it like that." I said defeated and feeling more stupid than ever to had thought I was really doing something.

That indeed was the truth. I hadn't thought past going to school for nursing because that was what I was convinced and certain I should do. Out of fear my relative would tell another relative what my major was, if asked how I was doing in school, I dropped all classes again and went back to the drawing board.

My third major was administration. After my third major, I felt my family get slowly disinterested in what I was doing. Why wouldn't they? I was slow to explain myself when asked "What happened to you going to school for so and so?" or "What you in school this time for?"

The question that got me the most was "So, when can we expect a graduation date?" I never had an answer for that so I stopped broadcasting my career moves. I wasn't sure if what I was going to do was for certain and I was deeply ashamed. I just wanted to make my mom, family, and even at one point, my step-father proud of me. I was seeking their validation. I wanted to be someone my siblings would want to look up to. I needed to know that I was doing the right thing by everyone else's standards; I did not dare to have a mind of my own.

Asetta Ramsey

I started school at 19. But four years later at 23, I was still a freshman no further than when I first started. I was working at a very biased job that I hated and wanted out of. I just wanted to be accepted there, I just wanted to fit in. I was tired of never having a place where I felt I belonged. After dropping my classes for the umpteenth time, I considered that if I couldn't figure out a career maybe I could use help in doing so.

I decided I was going to join the Navy.

Wanting to join the Navy was the most irrational, most bizarre thing I could have thought I could do. After consulting with my godmother and her husband who was an active member in the Navy, I thought it was in my best interest to do it. I witnessed friends who didn't know what to do with their lives join one of the special forces. Joining any of the special forces forced them to be somebody and changed their paths for the better, forever. That was what I so desperately wanted, to transform and change the path of my life forever. Within a couple of weeks of deciding that this was what I wanted to do, I set up an appointment with a recruiter who gave me the rundown on all and everything I would have to do. We talked about what was expected of me, the dedication of what it took to be in the Navy, and what boot camp basically was all about.

I walked in there ready to walk out a Navy recipient and instead, I walked out a convinced black girl from the Bronx that I wasn't with the shits. The Navy was officially out of the question. The fact of someone having authority over me treating me anything less than a person was something I'd familiarized with and knew all too well. I wasn't tolerable of upper management treating me in that fashion, so, I knew I couldn't tolerate any belittling from drill sergeants, no matter how much I would try to hide it. All the physical hardship I'd have to endure, I had to be honest with myself, I

CHAPTER THREE

wasn't strong enough for it. I let the excitement of doing something, the illusion of great achievements, get the best of me again.

I thought joining the Navy meant traveling the world, getting special treatment everywhere I went, and gaining great honors being a humanitarian with the compassion to care and provide for communities with struggling needs. The possibility of war never crossed my mind. Major 3rd world catastrophism never crossed my mind. Being equipped in using firearms never applied to me. Making a better life than the one I was living was all that mattered, but dying for thousands if not millions of people who would never know I existed, unless I was dead if that, made all the difference. I gained a new level of respect for all people who fought in all services and attached a new charm of disappointment to my bracelet of insecurities. I couldn't find the strength to be strong enough to get past the mental sacrifice it took to be America's hero. That reality was too real for me.

Failure was my biggest fear. Always had been, always felt like it would be. The greater my fear of not being able to choose a career to fall into, the closer failure got to knocking at my door, the deeper my footing sunk into my neighborhood's quicksand. I began to partake in illegal activities, get paid quick schemes, all while changing my job search to jobs that offered benefits. I needed security and if I couldn't find a career I loved, I at least needed a job with great benefits that I could learn to love that offered stability. I let thoughts of college fall back and decided to take time off, while I desperately searched for a better job. If I was ever to return back to college I wanted to be firm in the career I chose, that way I could follow and see it all the way through.

That year I took off from school, a couple of months later I got fired from my job at a check cashing store for getting food while on the clock without authorization. A long story on how that happened. I was unemployed the next day. I was relieved a little because I no longer had to deal with my old manager or the biased company, but I was also saddened because I gave them three years of my life and I did not know what my next move was. Now normally, and it's sad to say, when most people who come from similar backgrounds as I, get fired or laid off, unemployment becomes somewhat of a luxury. Some people love to stay home and collect unemployment. After two weeks of staying home and getting much needed rest, I didn't want to be home anymore. My friends who I enjoyed hanging out with all had jobs so I couldn't talk to them. The friends and family I knew that didn't work either were so accustomed to unemployment that living off of three to 400 dollars a week was satisfying enough to get by on or simply were on other assistance programs beside unemployment that made them lazy to where they did not care to work at all. Either way I had made the decision that I was not one of them. Now don't get me wrong there is nothing wrong with using government assistance to help you get on your feet. There is a problem to me however when people use the government's assistance as their common ground, never letting go to find their own footing in this world.

It killed me to watch my mother day in and day out working while I stayed home. I couldn't just lay around and do nothing, my mother's constant pushing through for her kids taught me that. I continued to dabble into illegal money activities with my banking accounts until I got caught up and ended up owing the bank. The so-called friends I did my dirt with disappeared on me leaving me to fend for myself. I had to come up with the money to settle the debt created in my account, or suffer the consequences behind it, possible jail time. I didn't want to ruin my name, create a criminal

CHAPTER THREE

background, or sabotage my credentials any further before I truly got the chance to use them. I took ownership of my wrong doings and began the process of paying gratuity out of the weekly stipend I received from unemployment. Doing so left me broke, with enough money to do my hair and feed myself only. I cried at my pathetic life, I hated living like this. I began to get up early and search for new job openings. I attended workforce interviews that were based upon my working experiences for the next four months.

December 19, 2013, I got the call that would change my life drastically. A human resource representative for a private hospital called me with a job offering to become an employee at one of their locations that I could not refuse. The position was to be a tray passer and I happily accepted no hesitation at all. This was a major game changer and huge accomplishment for me. I applied every year for three years to this specific hospital while working at my old job and I finally broke through. Not only was I no longer going to be unemployed, but I was going to be working for a job that offered me benefits and a union. I would be set for life. I had no intentions of leaving this job what so ever, why would I? I was young with a real job I could be proud of.

I shared the good news with my mom, friends, and family. My mom was super ecstatic that I'd gotten into the union once I passed probation. She also worked for the same private hospital and knew how hard I'd work to get in. We reminisced on how many rejection letters I received in the mail, and despite it all I kept on applying. She tried her hardest to pull some strings to get me in but since she was once a delegate, (a representative for workers who had issues presented against managers based off certain rules and regulations), no manager would help her help me get a job from within. This hospital was the hardest place to get into, but mommy expressed to me how proud she was of me for not giving up despite the setbacks. I thanked her for always pushing me and offering words of encouragement, even when I felt like giving up. We embraced for what seemed like hours.

I closed my eyes and was instantly returned to a childlike state wrapped in mommy's arms as the tears rolled down, she held me tighter. It felt so good to feel like a kid again. I missed being held like that pressing my head so close to her chest I could feel her heart beat. It has always been her and me ever since I could remember. We slow danced in our empty apartment to Luther Vandross's *Superstar*. Nothing was more important to me than this moment we shared in all our circumstances.

"I love you so much mommy." I said, looking up at her.

"I love you more Asetta." She said wiping the tears from my face.

"I really dooo!" she sang in unison with Luther.

I laughed as I placed my head back in her chest, she sang the whole song to me. I felt her teardrops on my shoulder, but I never looked up, I just held her tighter. I immediately returned back to an adult to care for her.

"I'll always be here for you ma." I assured her.

"I know my star." she replied.

Chapter Four

"If I give them the <u>POWER</u> to <u>FEED</u> me, I also give them the <u>POWER</u> to <u>STARVE</u> me." – Steve Maraboli

By the time I started working at my dream job in the hospital that January of 2014, my mom and I lost our apartment on Burnside Avenue the summer of that year. Twelve years of memories we had to leave behind haunting the rooms we were raised in. The new family that would move in would never know we existed. If we were going to move this was not the way I wanted it to happen. I shed too many tears in this home, to many moments in this home; Candles we lit when the lights went out and the love we held on to survive. This home was ours. We had our golden years as well as hardening times here and we left fighting to the end, that had to mean something. Someone had to know we fought for our sanctuary.

I left every poem I've ever written on the hardwood floor in the closet of my room. I left it there to let my home know that I loved it no matter what. I left it there to let the other family know I existed here once. I refused to be erased from a home that will always have a piece of me. With no other family members to stay with as a whole, we had to move back to our old neighborhood I grew up in as a child. My grandmother resided in the Morrisania II apartments better known as the Brown building. She lived there since the building first opened its doors in July 1980. I reminisced on the cab ride there about the awesome childhood I had growing up in my grandmother's building. Pure, unfiltered, truly fun childhood, where being a kid meant playing outside and interacting with other kids in my age group from the building and neighborhood.

    We played tag, relay race, hot potato, red light green light 123, doorbell ditch, hopscotch, double dutch, and man hunt. If you fought someone in the back, you used your hands and feet, and if you lost and wanted revenge, you retaliated with some clever trap to get that person the next day. You could look forward to tomorrow's, no one reached for a gun to blow you away. The Browns was popping. It was truly its own building of neighbors that were more like family within its community. The browns gave children like me love, character, strength, and spunk. The Browns gave me so much to anticipate, so much to do. The building sponsored dances by Ms. Peaches, we had a computer lab, candy store, and recreation room. My mom told me when she was a child growing up there they even had a library once.

    In the summer, they fed us through what we called free lunch in the community room. Free lunch is a free summer meals program that provides breakfast and lunch to kids. Every year on the building's opening anniversary, we celebrated by having, "Brown Building Day." On that day we barbequed, were given free ice cream from the truck, popcorn, face painting, and cotton candy.

    My fondest memory in the building was when Halloween came around we had a huge party with a haunted house in the com-

CHAPTER FOUR

munity room. Talk about a childhood, mine was real. Looking back then and how things are now, kids today are raised far different from the childhood I had. My brother and sisters never got to experience what being a child and having a real childhood experience was all about.

Somewhere I guess after the 90's transitioned into the 2000's, technology took over and made children lazy. Video games meant constant hours of staying in the house and playing inside instead of playing outside. Something more powerful than that happened. As the building went through the years, and the community began to change, people that were in power who had control stopped caring in my grandmother's building. I feel that this not only happened to my building, but to all the communities in the Bronx.

People stopped caring about us.

They took our community centers and closed them, leaving the city's kids with nothing to look forward to and nothing to do. As we dreamed overtime of a life much better than ours, the role models that made it out were the dope boys who glamorized being hood rich, and living ghetto fabulous, which fueled the deteriorating neighborhoods.

The block was played hard on the corners. Robbing, stealing, and drug selling escalated. There really wasn't such a thing as fighting fair anymore and living to see another day. Words exchanged resulted in bullets flying soon after, leading to the up rise in killings. Girls turned innocent beauty into devious missions to entice men who had the money and controlled the blocks. No one was thriving, the Bronx was barely surviving. Pulling up to the building the first day since 11 almost brought me to tears. The building was sinking, but only I could see it. It was shorter than I remembered. It smelled rancid, and was no longer a vibrant atmosphere where children grew character. The lobby and outsides of the building crowded with men. Some of them were guys I grew up with and some I didn't know. They stood around drinking, smoking, and chilling.

The sad part was that in any proper neighborhood in any proper building, this was unacceptable. In my world, this was life. Walking into my grandmother's building and seeing a bunch of guys chilling didn't disgust me because all the buildings I grew up in or visited were like this, this was normal to me. It pleased me to see a bunch of brothers showing each other brotherly love. They were laughing, joking, listening to music, and enjoying each other's company. I'd rather see that everyday over a shootout where one of these brothers would never make it to the lobby the next day. There was enough of that outside on the streets. Glass colored candle wax stained the ground and stood in remembrance for a brother who would never come back.

Moving into my grandmother's apartment I was anything, but thrilled about it. I wasn't for sure if I wanted to stay there because I just absolutely hated what became of the area and the building itself. I felt like I was trapped in a prison. I watched women my age, my mom's age, my grandmother's age, who I've known for years become nothing more than sitting ducks to the building and its surroundings. I didn't understand how people could sit around all day and do nothing, but chill with the same people who didn't do anything but fight, argue, drink, and smoke. There were women my age who looked washed up and older than me. I made it my business working at my new job to always have something to do so that I didn't have to play the back, the front, the lobby, or in the

CHAPTER FOUR

building period. Moving in with my grandmother over the months also gave me a horrific revelation that I was not prepared to deal with. Two months in after the move I realized that my grandmother was severely depressed as well as severely alcoholic. I stopped coming to her house as I got older because I knew she was depressed and no matter how hard I tried my best to help get her spirits up, it didn't work so I stopped coming around. She only wanted to talk about dying and my aunt's passing, and seeing her sad and crying made me sad and cry. I didn't want to feel like that and so I began distancing myself until I was no longer coming around anymore.

My grandmother's husband was also once an alcoholic before she became one and when none of us came around because his actions were distasteful; she called our house all the time to tell my mom the events of what went down in her house between my uncle and him when they fought. My cousin Kendall moved out a long time ago due to similar reasons. What my grandmother failed to tell us and take responsibility on was that not only was she the enabler to her husband's problems, she was also drinking heavily too. I had no idea of what was really going on in their household until I got a taste of it for myself. It was like she became demon possessed. She grew horns and let out the stench of death from her mouth as she over performed and lashed out on our family. As the months digressed she got worse. I was bewildered and couldn't believe my eyes. My grandmother had been the master behind the madness all this time.

My uncle so used to this way of living disregarded her actions as he stepped over her on the floor to head outside. He was immune to it all. He had tried in his own words to tell us but we didn't get the picture until we saw it first-hand. I was hurt and angry. My grandmother's husband stopped drinking due to reasons unknown, but my grandmother did not. She was guzzling vodka like it was water. I had walked into her room one time to get a comb to do my hair and accidently dropped it and it slid under her bed. When I went to retrieve it, I found numerous empty bottles under her bed.

What has happened to her? I thought rushing out her room and forgetting the comb altogether. I was saddened and disgusted all at once.

"I know she will never get over auntie's death none of us will." I continued to talk to myself. I tried to talk to her after that, to help her, to get her help. She listened modestly with no intentions of taking any advice I offered, but her own. She was convinced that she was fine and didn't really need any help from anyone.

Her refusing help or advice made me angry. We began to argue all the time. The arguing got so bad it escalated to physical fighting a couple of times. She always aimed for my face and out of reflex, I hit her back. I was so ashamed of what I had done. I cried my heart out because I was not raised that way, and I would never think to do such a thing to any elder. I was a woman of respect, mannerism, and integrity. My grandmother pulled me out of character and for the rest of my stay, continued to pick fights with me. My grandmother specialized in calling me out my name, she talked about my father who she hated in front of me, and overall made me feel as if I wasn't her grandchild at all.

Favoritism had been her thing and played a huge role besides the arguing and fighting between us. She constantly gave me a hard time when doing anything for me compared to how she went out of her way, above and beyond for my uncle and cousin. That past resentment mixed in with our current problems made a cocktail

CHAPTER FOUR

for disaster. To keep me from going crazy I seized every overtime opportunity as much as possible at work. I worked 12-14 hours a day and by the end of my work scheduled I'd accumulated over 120 hours or more with overtime included. I was tired until I got my first $1,500.00 check. I had never made that amount of money in my life. My check was twice the amount I made at my previous job. Once I realized that I had the opportunity to constantly make that amount of money, my job and making money became my number one priority.

    I didn't care if I was tired. I was getting paid and money became the epitome of my happiness. I began to afford things I couldn't before and I loved every minute of it. I brought a whole new wardrobe and having a wardrobe meant I needed new places to go, so I began to work hard and play harder. I would work a double go straight to the club, come home, get 2-3 hours of sleep, then do it all over again the next day. I was on such a high. This was what I wanted all along, to get paid, party, and have my own sense of independency. I was put in a position that enabled me to help my family if they needed something, and to provide for me to live happily. I didn't have to kiss anybody's ass for any favors or entertain any man to get what I wanted. I was good. I was complacent with my work and the hours I made. I knew this was where I wanted to be, and here was where I would stay.

    I wanted for nothing and something all at the same time. The main fact was that I wanted to get as far away from my living situation and out of the atmosphere I felt trapped in. I was working to buy my freedom, a way out of the real feelings I harvested deep inside. I was trying to create a happiness far from the reality I knew. Biggie once said, *"Mo money equals mo problems,"* and besides his poor times growing up in the hood, that was the truest thing I could relate to.

Asetta Ramsey

It seemed the more money I made the more problems I had. I wrote a check to buy a new happiness and it returned back to me null and void. I began to spiral out of control. The harder I worked, the harder I partied, the less I slept, the less I was home. Work wasn't fun for me anymore. My work ethics went unnoticed and taken for granted by my supervisors. I was pushing myself beyond limits that I knew of. I was running away from home physically, but emotionally the problems still lived with me. No matter how hard I worked, so hard that I spent nights in the hospital so that I didn't have to go home, the deeper I began to fall into the early stages of depression. Not only had I become depressed, I began to pick up a drinking problem. That made me hate my grandmother and myself more. I looked in the mirror and saw her in me.

When I did go home, the separation of my family mixed with the crowdedness of the house, was so thick, you could cut it with a knife. Every other day was a fight, an argument, another restless night.

All the glitters of my life weren't gold, nothing was solid.

My checks brought me clothes, the hottest club entries, bottle service, and trips to the south where I splurged on family and friends. Good credit brought me credit cards, and credit cards meant lavish purchases, but all these things were temporary. Once I spent the money I had to make more. I was tired and exhausted, but I didn't know how to stop.

I really didn't want to stop either, I lived for money. I praised, glorified, and served the almighty dollar bill. Money ruled me, and I was a slave to it. Money created a new lifestyle I couldn't really afford unless I worked hard for it. Without money, I was nothing. Money validated me on life's ladder of luxuries I couldn't afford otherwise. Money allowed me to escape everything I did not

CHAPTER FOUR

want to deal with. Even if it was temporary, I would give my all just to keep it that way. That was just it, I gave more than my all and my body was telling me in ways I ignored. My health became increasingly worse. I no longer slept, I could only sleep in 10-15 minute intervals. My eyesight became partially blurred, I suffered from excruciating migraines, and constant drastic mood swings.

    I was overcome with a great sense of sadness. Deep down in my soul I had this feeling that was proving to be more real every day. Money can only buy you an illusion of happiness, but money overall can't buy you happiness. I had what I thought I wanted, but I still wasn't quite happy or where I thought I should be having access to the kind of money I did. I was still missing out on something. Money fed me, but overtime it also began to starve me. I gave money the power to feed my ambitious desires and with that same power I allowed money to deprive me of any, and all, satisfaction and happiness. I was left starving, even dying inside, as I struggled to find limitless happiness in my life.

Asetta Ramsey

Chapter Five

"At a <u>CERTAIN POINT</u> in our lives, we <u>LOSE CONTROL</u> of what's happening to us, and our lives become <u>CONTROLLED</u> by <u>FATE</u>. That's the world's <u>GREATEST LIE</u>."

–The Alchemist by Paulo Coelho

    Emptiness took over my soul for an entire year as I continued the rat race of partying hard and working harder and vis a versa. My job, my place of employment that brought me the most joy in caring for people who were worse off than me, became a place I no longer wanted to be. My patients weren't at fault for that feeling. I truly loved the patients I cared for. I loved my position as a tray passer serving food to patients and their loved ones. It brought me great joy, in fact the only joy. The thought that in a place of hurt and misfortune, I had the power to offer a warm smile and kind words that impacted someone's life in a special way, all while offering food to nourish their soul and bodies, made me feel that much of a better person. I've always had a passion for people, but my job outside of my patients no longer served a purpose to me.

Asetta Ramsey

My department was the issue. Once I stepped off the elevator, the aura of my department was so vile and loathsome; I could barely find the strength to stomach the day. My home problems only got worse, so it was evidently no surprise when my home problems showed up promptly and punched in at work with me. My shortcomings and imperfections began to show in my appearance and attitude. I was deeply depressed and no one noticed enough to ask if I was okay. I was only noticed enough by associates who discussed the topic of my uniform. I walked the hallways passing smiling faces that turned their noses up, calling me dirty and dingy once my back was turned. Most nights I didn't make it home until 10:30 or 11:00 at night. I was too tired to wash my clothes by hand, and it was too late to go to the laundromat.

I only had enough energy to lay down at night and get up in the morning. Even in doing that it became harder to do. The closest of associates, I called friends, loved me and laughed in my face as if they saw no error in me, only to gossip about me when I wasn't around. My department ran an elite gossip mill, the biggest of the entire hospital, I believed. The best of the worst rumors spread off lips into eager ears ready to receive and recycle. Any and everyone's business was over analyzed and dissected only to be put to light for judgement, slander. I had no shame in telling people what kind of background I came from, especially the associates I considered friends. It was the principal of people, I considered friends, taking sensitive information told from me out of confidence being used against me, to sabotage my character and ridicule me for being disadvantage.

That hurt me the most and to make matters worse because I couldn't lash out, lashing out meant jeopardizing my lively hood, I had to tolerate being sneakily dissed and bullied by associates

CHAPTER FIVE

who openly expressed dislike for me just as I did to them. My life was opened to them and used as a cheat sheet for their advantage to push my buttons and defile me. I couldn't take another step into work or hear another gossip. I was done pretending it didn't bother me because I had feelings. I was done faking being painless. I cried constantly on the serving floors and in the stair cases.

What had I done to them to deserve this? I didn't deserve this.

Nobody deserves to feel or be treated like this. I was chosen for this though, the burn and hurt that was sewn and sealed on my heart. I carried the weight like the woman who bore the A on her chest in the Scarlet Letter, in abandoning silence. I was no longer spiraling into depression. I was climbing into bed and sleeping with it. My mind never stopped racing, my thoughts kept running. I was thinking and questioning, thinking and questioning.

What am I doing? Where am I going?

I had no clear idea on what I wanted to do, how I would achieve such goals when I couldn't afford schooling. I was stuck in a neighborhood I felt would consume my life and I had no help from anyone on how to get out of it. Everyone I asked help from with my problems had an idea or a suggestion on how to fix it, but no one could provide me with an answer. I needed a solution when all I was getting was endless frustrations.

I hated math, but that feeling you get when you get the answer correct on your own is all that matters. That correct answer made me like math for a brief split second of a moment because I understood it. That's what I was searching for, an agreement and understanding of me and life. Why did I have things I thought mattered, but still nothing to show for all my hard working that was valuable? Why does who I want to be in life, who I feel I am inside, not come out and show on the outside right now? Why am I not satisfied with where I was in life anymore? The answers were not adding up or making sense. Overthinking the decisions, I made in my life overtime, some poor decisions, mixed in with the current depressing state of my mind drove me crazy. I became increasingly bothered, capital C.R.A.Z.Y. I had no vision on how to change my circumstances.

I was no longer satisfied with where I was in life anymore. I was uncomfortable and no longer wanted to be complacent with the fate of my life. Wanting to get away from all that was bothering me I did what I knew best, I decided to hit a club up for good drinks, music, and fun. I called myself going out to one of the hottest club/ lounge spot with my cousin and instead of taking my mind off my problems and enjoying myself, I began reflecting on my life again and then it dawned on me, the straw that broke the camel's back. In my first year of working I made over $45,000.00 and walked away with a $10,000.00 payout in taxes. Here I was in the club looking beautiful and I couldn't even tell myself where the money went, or what I spent it on. I couldn't even afford to party with my cousin that night, yet I blew ten thousand dollars and had nothing to show for it. I cried like a baby at the thought. Tears began to fall hard and heavy as I let it all sink in. I was still a freshman in college who never even touched ten thousand ever in any form of cash, let alone tax money and I didn't put it to use by starting a business, or investing in something. I was struggling because I ran through money just as fast as I received it. I should have been more established than what I was.

This was not what I wanted anymore. As I got up to put my drink down, I straightened my dress and walked out the club, away from the party life for a good while. I declared to myself that I no

CHAPTER FIVE

longer wanted a job and I knew why. I wanted a career, not just a nine to five anymore. I wanted a career that was meaningful to me, a career that had purpose. I wanted to wake up and love what I did for the rest of my life. When you love what you do it doesn't feel like work because it becomes your passion. I wanted a passionate career. Panic set in instantly after coming to this realization. I felt like this revelation was a little too late, leaving me pressed for time. I was running out of time to be successful. I still didn't know what I wanted to do or what direction to go in. I sank deeper into depression. I just wanted to be successful and when it was all said and done, I truly wanted to be happy.

I've been living all lies all this time. My life was nothing, but that of chasing illusions and fantasies that did not help or benefit me. I was a failure, my biggest fear and that was the only thing that ran true in my life. Pain and suffering never surpassed me, it was the best life had to offer me I was convinced. I could no longer carry on. I accepted fate and according to fate, failures deserved to die, and so I knocked on life's door and handed in my keys.

Asetta Ramsey

YOU ARE WHAT YOU BELIEVE

Lost.
No closer to the beginning than touching the end.
I've tried to stand tall,
while chains on my ankles weigh me down.
What is my purpose?
All this pain has got to amount to something one day.
I want to be great, but what is so special about me?
They say you are what you believe.
I believe I can be great, but what's so special about me?
When my dreams are so far-fetched from my reality.
I'm too old now; it's too late for me.
I've searched to find
reflecting the image that's staring back at me.
FAILURE, open and exposed for all to see.
I'll end it now,
With the DEATH OF ME.
Too WEAK to fight back,
Too ENSLAVED to be SET FREE.
They say you ARE what you BELIEVE....

-*Asetta Ramsey*

Chapter Six

"You have got to __LOSE__ your __MIND__, just to __FIND__ your __PEACE__ of __MIND__." – Jhené Aiko

    I sat in the chair in the counselor's office as she made numerous phone calls to numerous people. I was tired, extremely tired, but in all my tiredness there was a slight sense of relief somehow. I told her what I told nobody. I told her my plans to jump in the Hudson River, the promise of death on my life I was trying to fulfill. I told her of the confusion and loneliness I was drowning in, the money and random trips out the state I couldn't account for. I told her the details of my home situations, the overall stress and bullying at work, and about the constant need to get away from everything and disappear. I told her about the recent sudden surges of panic and fear that came over me, causing me to have trouble breathing and sweaty palms.

    "You were experiencing an anxiety attack Asetta, did you know that?" the counselor asked me.

    "No," I said to her while thinking. So that's what an anxiety attack feels like.

Asetta Ramsey

After another ten minutes of her calling numbers and speaking to other people, she hung up and proceeded to speak with me.

"So, I just got off the phone with a good friend of mine who suggested a behavior center in Long Island, Queens. How do you feel about me sending you there, Asetta?" she looked at me intently as she leaned over on her desk.

"Afraid." I told her as I struggled to make eye contact with her, "To go to a mental institution means I'm crazy. right? I may never be able to go home once I go there, right? I'll get doped up on medicine while doctors do all sorts of experiments on me, right?" my words lingered in the air as I waited for her voice to break the silence.

The counselor smiled a little, "It's not going to be at all like that Asetta, I promise."

She continued, "First and foremost, going to a behavior center doesn't mean you are necessarily crazy. This place can offer you time away from the problems you are facing so that you can talk to teachers and doctors who specialize in mental health, people who can show you the protocol to getting back in check, and overall healthy stability."

"I suggest this place to you as well because I think you need a mental vacation." The counselor smiled wider while talking, I could tell she was looking for a smile back.

"Not only is this facility highly recommended, the best part is that you'll be surrounded by other college students. This place was specifically designed for college students coming from different schools in New York."

Her mentioning that made me feel more at ease. The counselor must have known she broke through on selling me this place because she stood to her feet and sat down next to me as she held my hand.

CHAPTER SIX

"Asetta, I think you would love this, but most importantly I think that you need this. Considering everything that you have been through, you need time away from operating your life by yourself. Doesn't that sound good?" There was that condescending tone I wanted to correct her on, but right now all I was searching for was peace of mind. I wanted the thoughts I was having to stop. I needed space, somewhere to go and I was more than ready to stop everything from moving just to get time and space to myself.

I was tired in all physical and emotional aspects of my life. I needed the rest and if I had to go to a mental behavior center to get it, I accepted what was to come. I knew of nothing else to do, nowhere else to go, I was as ready as I could ever be. With the stroke of her pen and dial of her finger, the ambulance, my horse and carriage, were on their way to wisp me away. As they carried me on the stretcher to the truck outside, I noticed how bad it was snowing for the first time. As the thick flakes fell on my face I wanted right then and there to jump in a huge pile of snow and make snow angels, the innocence of the child I wanted to come back to me.

It took three hours to get to the Long Island Jewish Hospital. Once there, the instant fear crept in as I pulled my hoodie over my face. Sick people were everywhere. I grabbed a face mask as I was escorted through the emergency room bending corners and walking down hallways of ill people. This maze of walking down corridors and turning corners seemed to never want to end until it did. I paused, stopped dead in my tracks as we approached a wing in the hospital that was all too quiet. I pulled the drawstrings of my hoodie tight to my face. I needed it to squeeze me tight so that I knew that what was happening was real.

"It's ok, Asetta." The EMS guy told me as he walked back to stand behind me to watch me go on.

Asetta Ramsey

"He thinks I'm going to run." I said to myself. "I almost did." I responded reassuringly.

I had nowhere to run though. I'd exposed myself and now I was somewhere far from home with nowhere to hide.

"Ok." I said to the EMS guy as I breathed in and exhaled out, it all came down to this.

I walked up to the counter and stared at the floor. I didn't know where else to look until the nurse began to speak to me.

"Hi Asetta," the nurse said to me, "We've been expecting you."

I stared back down at the floor, feeling like a shameful puppy that looks down when its owner asks if he spread the garbage all over the floor.

"I know that you're nervous and maybe even a little afraid. I want to reassure you that you're in good care and everything is going to be alright. Can you take the hoodie off your head, please, so that I can see your face?"

I did as I was told, but I refused to remove the face mask, so she let me rock with that.

"Do you mind stretching your arm out so that I can place these ID bracelets on you?" I watched her as she placed the id bracelet on and then another colorful bracelet that was much thicker and harder to take off.

"The crazy bracelet." I said to myself wanting to laugh and cry out hysterically because I just couldn't believe my eyes.

"Now that that's all done would you so kindly follow me to the next room, where we can get you settled in?"

I chuckled at the words "settle in." This all seemed so unreal, but it wasn't fake, this wasn't a dream, this was real and happening. In the next room stood a man at a table where I was

CHAPTER SIX

given a gown, a blanket, and a large plastic bag for all my belongings. I changed my clothes and handed the guy my bag of belongings.

"Now all you have to do is wait for the specialist to see you and escort you to tower 1. You're very lucky though because they just built that wing and it's really nice. It looks just like a hotel."

I smiled a little because I was happy to know that. My interpretation of a mental institution was dark and dank, grey even looking. Where the hallways were filled with crying and screaming patients and shit being thrown at the staff or across the walls. I pictured a mental institution no different than how I viewed a prison. Before I sat down to wait, I asked if I could have something to eat. I was starving and my mouth was dry and thirsty. I was rewarded with two dry turkey sandwiches no mayo and apple juice. I scoffed it down wanting more and before I could get the chance to ask, a woman was escorted in the room extremely irate and ready for war with the staff. She stood in the center of the floor and with her bold loud mouth and commanded anyone to come get "some of this" as her sister tried desperately to calm her down.

Everyone was at attention. The security guards urged her to calm down as she proceeded to tear her gown off her body exposing her breast. She began spitting and yelling obscenities. Out of nowhere one of the staff members grabbed me and two other girls where we stood watching in awe, to a second room.

"I want you ladies to stay here for your safety," she said quickly as she shut the door.

"Oh shit! That was crazy, right!?" one girl said to me still shocked.

'Crazy!? No girl! Have you looked around at where we are? She's perfectly sane, she's acting like right where she belongs.' I wanted to respond to her, but I opted for a shy smirk and a, "Yeah, that was crazy."

After about eight minutes in the other room we no longer heard the irate woman. I don't know what they did to her, but the silence of the unit returned quickly making me anxious to know how they were able to tame such a big out of control woman in those few minutes.

One of the nurses returned back to our room and with a warm smile said

"The coast is clear; we're going to keep you ladies in this room, the specialist is here to speak with you. I know you ladies are tired so we will move things quickly so you guys can get some rest okay?"

"Ok." We said in unison.

"Aseeta Ramsey," the nurse said nonchalantly.

"Asetta!" I corrected her. "AH-SET-TA," I said reassuringly.

That was a pet peeve of mine, I hated when my name was pronounced or spelled wrong. My name was so easy to say and spell to me if people took the time to want to pronounce it correctly. My name was said without such care. I, at least, would have appreciated if she had asked if she was saying it right before or after she bluntly said it wrong. Noticing the irritation of pronouncing my name wrong she humbly apologized which made me feel bad for scolding her.

"It's okay," I said walking out the door behind her.

I was escorted to another room where the specialist sat. She was medium built with a short haircut and droopy eyes. She looked like she needed sleep maybe even more than me, I was convinced.

"Hello." The specialist said as she pulled out her paperwork.

CHAPTER SIX

I searched the floor again, that overwhelming feeling returning as I twirled my fingers and crossed my feet.

I am being judged, were the thoughts that were filling up the hallways in my mind. Clipboards and paper work meant trapping and tracking my thoughts, emotions, and behaviors in her certified files. I was leaving paper trails, and paper trails meant I signed a binding contract to names and conditions that labeled and categorized me into bondage I could never escape from. Into bondage that I did not want to define me. This experience would stick and follow me no matter where I went.

Is this better than being dead? The tears began to roll. I tried to catch them before they fell. Unaware that I was going off on a tangent in my mind, the specialist had been watching me since "hello," she handed me a box of tissues.

"Why are you here, Asetta?" she asked tilting to meet my bowed head. Still looking at the floor I replied

"I'm tired of living, I can't get a break, I'm lost, I'm tired of being poor, and I wanted to kill myself today."

The specialist began scribbling away and I let out such a deep sigh of defeat, she moved closer to me. I began to cry uncontrollably right into another anxiety attack.

"What the fuck!?" I thought to myself as I told her I couldn't breathe.

"Calm down, Ms. Ramsey!" The specialist held my hand as she knelt on the floor to meet my face.

"Breathe in, exhale out, and breathe in again Asetta. Listen to me." I stared at her, squeezing her hand tighter trying to do as I was told.

I felt ashamed, embarrassed, and weak. Two staff members rushed in with a cup of water and an oxygen mask to assist me. The attack left me fragile and empty.

"What were you thinking about Asetta before the attack happened?" the specialist asked me still on her knees rubbing my back, after I calmed down.

"What am I doing here?" I stared at her helplessly, "Why is this happening to me? Why is my life out of control? I can't answer those questions; why can't I answer those questions?"

"You are severely depressed, Asetta," she said getting up off her knees.

"You're so depressed your ability to cope with the life you're living, you are abandoning it. You've stopped living emotionally, physically, and mentally. I'm going to ask you a question," she continued, "And I don't want you to get offended, remember I am here to help, I am on your side."

I waited for the question to be asked.

"Asetta, when is the last time you showered and took care of your personal hygiene?"

"Bitch what!?" I thought to myself, but my facial expression told her anyway, because she repeated, "Remember I am here to help." I looked at her with disgust.

"What do you mean when's the last time I took a shower? I," and then there was nothing.

"I," and still nothing as I stared at the ceiling this time trying to remember my last shower. The fact that I had to think about it was making me upset. I leaned back in my chair as I humbled myself down to size and came to what sense I had left.

"I, I, I can't remember." I said as I shook my head in disbelief.

It had to have, at least, been a week, if that, since I showered. My condition became that much realer as I let the fact of what I just said sink in.

CHAPTER SIX

"Asetta I know this is all traumatizing to you, but I need you to remain calm okay?
One of the signs of depression besides anxiety is lack of personal hygiene."

"I have an odor is what you're saying," I interjected, "This is not like me!" I said puzzled.

"I believe this is not you," she responded, "This is why you are here, this is why I am here. You are unstable and we are here to help you get through this and better."

We talked about everything I was going through like I did with the counselor. After an hour of dissecting my brain and emotions, the specialist's job with me was complete.

"We're all done here Asetta, your room is ready and in the next five minutes, you will be escorted to the Zucker Hill Behavior Center. I know that with the special doctors we have here you'll leave feeling much better than you came in. I just need you to sign these dotted lines and then we can send you on your way to some much-needed help."

Help, help, help. help me please. the words echoed in my head. I walked out the room and straight to the nurses' desk where I asked if I could call my mom before I left. My mom had no idea where I was. I called her crying, trying to explain everything to her. My mom stopped me in my pleading to her and said, "Asetta bow your head, raise your hand and repeat after me."

I stood on the phone tears and snot falling as she prayed over me and repeated every word she asked of me. I love my mother with every inch of my heart, I listened to her cry from her heart as she began praying louder over me, making me cry even more for putting her through this.

"I love you Asetta you hear me!? Mommy loves you and

the devil is a liar, don't you ever forget that. You are my child, the child of God and you are going to be alright, you are covered and I plead the blood over your heart, your body, and your mind. I declare and command it in the name of Jesus!"

I entered the van with expectations of the unexpected. It took all of eight minutes to get to the facility, and as I stepped off the van and into the building, my heart began to break. I walked down a long hallway leading to double doors that needed electronic id clearance to get in. Once in, I reached a second pair of doors that required the same as the first. This place was extremely locked down. I was greeted by another nurse of the facility along with a staff aide. I gave my bag to the staff aide and followed the nurse into her room. Before I even got the chance to sit down the staff aide called out to me.

"Your shoes as well Ms. Ramsey."

"I have to give my boots to you?" I asked a little angry. "Why?" I was confused and wanted to know.

"It's a part of the procedure, there's no shoes allowed except when you're allowed to step out for fresh air, we return them to you and take them back once inside."

She continued, "We do however provide socks with traction at the bottom of them…"

"…patient socks" I interjected, "the green socks with the ridges on the bottom."

"Yes." She confirmed as she stood there with her hands out waiting anxiously for my boots.

I rolled my eyes as I took each boot off to hand to her. This was unbelievable, I couldn't be trusted with my shoes on my feet.

I traded my clothes in for a hospital gown and my boots for socks. This was the transition. I went from serving patients to be

CHAPTER SIX

coming one. It was so dehumanizing for me because I loved and genuinely felt sorry for the patients I served, and now woe is me. There was no one who loved me here, no one who cared, no one to hurt and feel sorry for me. These were strangers serving the strange like me. I wanted to cry so bad, but I decided to hold it down until I reached my room. After getting checked out for the millionth time and checked in, I was given a brief tour of the facility up until we reached my room. I must say I was impressed. The facility did look just like a hotel like I was told. There was a huge lounging area, floor to floor carpeting, a piano room, library area, game room, kitchen, and dining area. I had to share my room, but it had hardwood flooring and the bathroom looked like a sauna. Everything was touch-sensitive to turn on. I especially loved the lighting. There were so many dimmed lights the scene was just set to be serene. I was told the rules and regulations and then left alone for the night.

    My roommate hadn't shown up yet so I was able to shower in peace. After showering I climbed into bed. Lying in bed was the best feeling ever and the worst at the same time. I dreamt of the day I would have my own room, better yet, my own bed. I'd slept on hard floors, couches, and air mattresses for so long, I forgot what it felt like to sleep in a bed that was all mine. This moment felt so good.

    Tears rolled and they never stopped that night. I was lying in a real bed, but look at where I am. I looked out the window, noticing the high gates and barbed wire surrounding this place. I imagined that this is what the first night of prison must have felt like when the person in jail heard the cell doors lock down.

    You belong to this place now; this place is your home. I cried myself to sleep.

Day one I slept, I mean I slept like I never slept before. Two staff aides tried to get me up to eat, but I didn't want to. I wanted to sleep so they let me be. Another staff aide checked in on me in the afternoon to let me know that the doctors wanted to see me.

"Tomorrow please," I begged her. I wasn't ready for the examining and picking of my brain or the experiments used to dissect me, I just wanted to rest. I slept for so long that when I awoke in the middle of the night to use the bathroom, I immediately collapsed back in the bed from dizziness. I knew that my sugar dropped a lot, luckily for me I managed to sneak a piece of candy that I tucked in my drawer. I didn't budge after that, I didn't dare to move. I laid down, closed my eyes and went back to sleep.

Day two was a little better than the first. I got up, ate breakfast, and met with the doctors and their assistances to talk about my feelings. They told me about symptoms of Bipolar Depression and because they believed that that was what I was suffering from, they told me about the medicine they were going to start me with for in-treatment. I opposed the medicine, but because I had no other option, I followed the rules for taking it.

Throughout the day I participated in ice-breaker activities and was introduced to everyone that was there. In group sessions, we talked about the pain that led to the paths we chose. We identified triggers according to our conditions, what they meant, and how we would deal or get over them. We also talked about personal hygiene and the importance of keeping it at safe levels. I was still embarrassed and sensitive to the thought of me not showering and keeping groomed, but best believe the rest of my stay there I bathed three times a day. Any unsettling smell or at any sign of an itch, I immersed myself in soap and water. I was given my first Effexor pill right after the programs for the day were over. We were left the

CHAPTER SIX

rest of the day to talk on the time controlled phones they provided and amongst ourselves. I socialized for the most part until I found myself lounging in one of the chairs watching my surroundings. Then, I fell asleep. I awoke as early evening fell upon the center extremely hungry and groggy.

    I ate and returned to my spot on the couch in the lounge as I continued to watch people and socialize with other patients. I had never seen so many Asian and Indian people in one place. I thought of them as the smartest stereotypically speaking. In fact, with the exception of two other black students, it was only three of us there. As night began to fall, I watched as the staff called each person up to the counter to take their medicine. Some people took two to three pills while others like me only took one. I sat back observing speaking not a word as I let the medicine from the pill I swallowed run its course.

    Twenty minutes later I saw monsters come alive. Each person grew extremely sleepy rubbing their eyes as they began to drag their feet to their rooms one-by-one. I knew right then and there why I had slept so good and why I woke up so groggily and savagely hungry earlier, it was the medicine. We were turned into zombies walking roaming around at night aimlessly. We had nowhere to go, but to our beds. I examined my hands and feet as I watched myself walk to my room and into my bed. I wasn't in control of my feelings or body at this point, medicine and sleep was in control of me.

    I became more depressed as I climbed into bed. I wasn't that different from the other students that were here. We all came from a background of pain that was familiar. That pain was what brought us together to this specific place. All the people that I met here were in their own ways brilliant to me. Some students were musically talented, great writers, and true scholars. So, what did that say about me? My very good friend Stephanie told me once, as I cried in a corner at work to her, on a really down day, that the smartest greatest people come from some line of insanity, some broken deep dark past. The reason why people like that struggle is because they are fighting to be great. I loved Stephanie for times like that because one, they were rare she barely liked people, and two, her words uplifted my spirits. No one was really crazy here I believed. We were smart, brilliant, geniuses who went crazy trying to fight for something. We emotionally detached ourselves from everything because we were underneath so much pressure from being misunderstood. It made perfect sense when we as misfits came together to share our stories.

  We were not emotionally strong like we either were told to be or judged for not being. We let the influences of how people took our indifferences, the things that made us unique and gave us our own authentic identity, try to make us fit into what "was right." I accepted that night that I did not fit anywhere I tried because I was different. I didn't want the pills I took to define me either. I did not believe that this was the overall remedy to my problems. I wanted to heal the pain and not suppress it. For me that was what I felt the medicine was doing for me, suppressing my emotions because I didn't feel anything good. I was sleepy and hungry. I didn't feel sad much, but I knew for sure I wasn't happy. I needed the correct dosage that would help me find me. I laid in bed another crying night until I fell asleep. Searching for the answers in my mind to fix what I was feeling. This pain was different though, this pain wasn't coming from my mind, it was lodged in my heart. No amount of medicine could fix that. This pain needed to be held, to be felt to be understood. I was convinced that what I really needed more was hands on open heart surgery.

Chapter Seven

"The number 3 refers to the TRINITY, and means that you are receiving DIVINE PROTECTION, HELP, and GUIDANCE. 3 is an Angel number sign that you have a close connection to JESUS, the son in the holy trinity. THREE IS THE NUMBER OF RESSURECTION."

-Google Search & The Bible

Day three wasn't like any other day. I wish I could sit here and share every day of my stay there after, but the truth of the matter is that day three was all that mattered. Nothing else mattered or existed to me because on that day my life changed for forever. I remember feeling hopeless, sad, and lost, but most of all lonely. The kind of loneliness that allows you to step out of perspective and question all the people that surround you. The kind of loneliness that allows you to feel the emptiness inside of you. There was no one to turn to.

What was I going to do? I replayed all the decisions I had made in my life and began to analyze them.

"I have been alone for a while," I thought.

I could never explain to anyone who actually listened to me the visions I had seen for myself. When I spoke on my behalf I was met with rejection. When I sought out validity from the things people told or wanted me to do, I rejected myself worth and feelings just to please others. Try as I might I could not make peoplee happy for me. Come to think of it, I never really supported me or cheered me on in what I wanted to do. I was always all alone. As I began to tear, one of the staff members walked in and handed me a composition notebook and a pen.

I sat on my bed unsure of my next move from here. I tried to think and think hard, but for the first time ever in my life I could think of nothing, my mind was blank. I began to weep in defeat. The hell outside I wanted to be saved from was no better than the hell here I thought. I was stuck in neutral, no better off than before. I was helpless, hopeless, and dead once again. I was drowning in my biggest fears of being trapped and the worst, being a failure. I spread my worksheets from the activities I participated in, along with sheets pertaining to my condition, across the bed as I read everything that I'd done there so far. My heart was heavy and hurting. I had nothing and nobody.

Where was my God? I didn't know.

Why am I even here? I didn't know the answer to that either.

Frustrated and desperate with nowhere to turn, I bowed my head and asked for help.

"Please help me, please help me, please help me....," I sobbed out.

I began to think of my mother, my siblings, my grandmother, my cousin, all the people that had ever loved me truly and I broke down. I crumbled, I teared, and I fell apart. I caved into the hollowness of me and in the midst of sobbing in my complete brokenness I heard my name called softly.

CHAPTER SEVEN

"Asetta..."

I looked up. I was sure I was hearing things because I was the only one in the room.

"My mind is definitely playing tricks on me," I said as I raised to my feet in fear.

"There's that voice they've been asking me have I been hearing other than my own, you want to show up now?!"

I raised my hands in the air and began to cry hysterically.

"Oh my God I'm crazy, I'm crazy, I'm going crazy, I'm hearing voices now!"

I circled the floor panicking.

I was sure I was going to run myself into an anxiety attack. I was sure that this time it would be different. This time my heart would burst, I was for certain that this time I would actually die.

"Asetta!"

My name was called louder, my body froze and I stopped dead in my tracks.

I didn't have an anxiety attack, my heart didn't burst, and I for certain didn't die. Instead a calmness came over me. The kind of calmness I instantly remembered that brought me back to when I took a walk in the Brooklyn Botanical Gardens with my boyfriend at the time. I was at total peace and serenity with him amongst the gardens' trail of flowers. I remembered that time because that was a very loving unforgettable time for me and this calmness that came over me felt like that experience times ten. I wasn't afraid of what I heard in that moment. My tears had instantly stopped. My body was still and I did not move because I was covered.

And out of the abundance of His heart God began to speak to me.

He said, "I am who I say that I am. I have never left your side. I have always been here for you even when you turned your back and stopped believing in me. I love you Asetta, don't you know that? I have been speaking to you all this time. The only reason why you have not been able to hear me is because you have been surrounded by so much noise. I am a God. I will not yell over the noise to get your attention. I needed to get you here because here there is peace and quiet. I needed to get you here to this very place, so that the only voice you can be influenced by is mine and mine alone. You heard me clearly the first time. You are not crazy or insane but you are loved by me. The very thing that you have been searching endlessly for has always been there, it has always been inside of you. I have placed it in you the day that I thought to create you. Use what I gave you…"

    I dropped down to my knees and began to worship God like I never worshipped Him before ever in my life. I had not believed in Jesus anymore and yet He spoke to me and He told me He loved me. As I laid on the hardwood floors crying my heart out, God began to pour into me. With every kiss, He showered on me, He showed and reminded me of all the times I prayed to Him as a child. How he answered my prayers through all my times of sadness and mistreatment. He was there all the time. When I thought I had nobody, I had Jesus. God tapped into memories in my mind I had not even known him to intercede in. All I could do was tell God how sorry I was and that I loved Him again. As I picked myself up off the floor, feeling no longer of emptiness but overflowing in love, I made a declaration that day that I was going to live. Not only was I going to live, but I was going to get out of here and never come back.

CHAPTER SEVEN

There was a spark in my soul that ignited and spread like wildfire. This, this surge of energy spread from my heart down my right arm, all the way to the very end of my fingertips. I had an insane ironically crazy urge to write. I felt the words rising up in me as I scrambled to reach for my composition notebook. There were so many words filling up inside of me, I was too afraid to wait a second longer to get them out for fear of losing them. I'd written like I never written before, like my life depended on it. It was all coming back to me, the rush, the adrenaline, the pure unfiltered love. I was brought back to how writing made me feel when I was eight. All the memories, the straining of beauty out of pain began to flood me. My words began breathing life into me as I bled over my pages. I didn't want this feeling to end. I had been searching for this for six years, my joie de vivre, my pursuit of happiness. Writing kept me grounded, full, and happy.

It was then that I realized that I had been unhappy because I had given up on my dreams, hopes, and aspirations as a writer. When I wrote I was unstoppable, powerful, important, brilliant. I had let negative influences stop me from doing the thing I was superb at, that I was gifted in, that was my heart's desire, to meet other people's expectations and the only one that hurt when doing so was me. Writing allowed me to be unscripted, unapologetic, the real me. The first thing I wrote was an apology letter to myself. I was truly sorry to me. How could I have doubted myself and abandon my talents just to be accepted, just to fit in?

I told myself that I would never allow anyone to turn me astray from the very thing God made special and specifically for me. I was born to be different, unique, and authentic. I wrote boldly, I dreamed widely, and I loved what I did unconditionally. Only those who thought less of what I did remained average and that is why I did not fit, why I did not belong.

    After writing the apology letter to myself, I wrote one to my mom, my Madre. Mommy was the only one besides my grandmama who never saw me anything short of the greatest writer they had ever known. I was my grandmother's Maya Angelou, my mother's Langston Hughes, above them both I was their Asetta Shakurah Ramsey, their most prized poet and writer. I needed to get out of here so that I could hug my mom and kiss my grandmama. They supported me and believed in me from day one. Then there was professor Stoute. I owed her the biggest thank you because she seen my potential and never let me forget it. Had it not been for her I would have never met the schools' counselor that sent me here. Most importantly I thanked God for not letting me kill myself and for interceding through all these people in my life. For having me run through this course of life I had to get lost in in order to be found.

    Things began to happen ridiculously fast after I got through all the poetry and journaling I could write. I began sharing my words aloud in group sessions throughout the rest of my stay. The response I got was nothing short of what I expected. I'd gotten many compliments and some people began to draw themselves near to me. I found myself uplifting and motivating everyone around me. I was shaking and moving with so much positivity and good spirits, I had even gotten a difficult patient that had not eaten for two days to come out of her room and speak. The staff kept asking me what I did to get her to move and even I really didn't know. All I could tell them was that I spoke to her from my heart. That feeling of helping and making other people feel good in their worst of moments like what God did for me on that third day, like what I

CHAPTER SEVEN

did for my sick patients at the hospital, made me feel so good.

I flashed back again to the days of Professor Sa-Rawla Stoute who seen the talent before I came to realization, I wanted to be the push to those who gave up like she was for me. Professor Stoute always pushed me to pursue a writing career and to speak.

She was right.

If there was one person, I should have listened to it was the teacher with the ponytail who wore glasses and always kept it real. I knew what I wanted to do and who I wanted to be in life, I had found my passion. Hitting rock bottom, losing my mind, and all control was a blessing in disguise. All the decisions I made and all the struggling I went through, and the entire negative backlash I got from people that were important to me, was a part of the preparation. I was being prepared for my moment of darkness. The moment where I would walk in alone and find the light of God. I found the key to happiness in my life; it was in God's love for me. In God's love for my talents and dreams. God revealed to me that I had his power and his strength to win victory over my life. The desire to write never left me. My love was still there hidden amongst the thousands of lost and abandoned stories, resting on the dirty bookshelf I left her on six years ago. Dreaming of the day I could possibly return to dig up the earth and claim the treasure that was rightfully mine.

__TODAY WAS THAT DAY.__

Asetta Ramsey

Epilogue

Some people have special gifts on their lives... Some people are singers blessed with voices to sing and entertain; some are artists and musically inclined and become famous for their talents... which I call favor on their lives. I believe that on March 11, 1990 the Lord blessed me with a baby girl like that. She was born only weighing 2lbs 3ounces at twenty-eight weeks. She was born premature, her due date of birth was supposed to be May 22, 1990. She was born before her time; she had to see the world earlier. I always felt something special about her... that I had to be more protective of her... as she grew older, I began to feel that she had a calling on her life... I knew that she had a talent in writing poetry- good stuff (the kind of stuff that a mother says... "Wow" these are my baby's words). That being said, I automatically said yeah... she's going to be a teacher one day...

It didn't happen... but... I never gave up on her. Sometimes you have to find yourself, your purpose. That takes a lot of praying and having a relationship with Jesus. I am happy to be a part of this journey with "MY STAR". She has found her calling. Her hands have been blessed with the 'Gift of Writing". I hope that this book and her future books will be a blessing to many lives that may be going through similar situations. Inspire them to never give up on the Lord, themselves, or their Dreams. No matter what you're going through you are not alone!

-Words from Mommy

www.ingramcontent.com/pod-product-compliance
Lightning Source LLC
Chambersburg PA
CBHW070938160426
43193CB00011B/1726